The Politics of Post-Suharto Indonesia

Coedited by
Adam Schwarz   Jonathan Paris

COUNCIL ON FOREIGN RELATIONS PRESS
NEW YORK

The Council on Foreign Relations, Inc., a nonprofit, nonpartisan national membership organization founded in 1921, is dedicated to promoting understanding of international affairs through the free and civil exchange of ideas. The Council's members are dedicated to the belief that America's peace and prosperity are firmly linked to that of the world. From this flows the mission of the Council: to foster America's understanding of its fellow members of the international community, near and far, their peoples, cultures, histories, hopes, quarrels and ambitions; and thus to serve, protect, and advance America's own global interests through study and debate, private and public.

From time to time books, monographs, and reports written by members of the Council's research staff or others are published as a "Council on Foreign Relations Book." Any work bearing that designation is, in the judgement of the Committee on Studies of the Council's Board of Directors, a responsible treatment of a significant international topic.

Council on Foreign Relations Books are distributed by Brookings Institution Press (1-800-275-1447). For further information on Council publications, please write the Council on Foreign Relations, 58 East 68th Street, New York, NY 10021, or call the Director of Communications at (212) 434-9400. Or visit our web site at www.foreignrelations.org.

Printed in the United States of America.

Library of Congress Cataloging-in-Publication Data

Post-Suharto Indonesia / edited by Adam Schwarz and Jonathan Paris.
p. cm.
Includes bibliographical references and index.
ISBN 0-87609-247-4
1. Indonesia. 2. International Politics.

KZ6373.E28 1999
327.1'17—DC21

98-23408
CIP

Contents

Foreword

ALTHOUGH ongoing economic, political, and social crises have kept Indonesia in the headlines for over a year, Southeast Asia's troubled giant remains poorly understood in the United States. This 17,000-island archipelago, extending over 3,000 miles from east to west, occupies a strategic location that connects the Arabian Sea and Indian Ocean to East Asia. The fourth most populous country in the world, Indonesia is home to as many Muslims as the entire Middle East/North Africa region. It is first among equals in the Association of Southeast Asian Nations (ASEAN), the nine-country regional grouping that is a key part of East Asia's prevailing balance of power. Indonesia's domestic turmoil, triggered by the collapse of the rupiah but rooted in profound and long-standing causes, is only now bringing the country the attention that its size and potential warrant.

This volume redresses the scarcity of relevant research on Indonesia available to U.S. policymakers, practitioners, and scholars. It is a product of a Council study group initiated by Council Fellow Jonathan Paris, who was joined by Adam Schwarz, the Council's 1997–98 Murrow Fellow, as codirector of the study group and the coeditor of this book. The authors focus on those areas that will be particularly nettlesome for Indonesia's new leaders: the economy, religion and ethnicity, civil society, and the military. The result of their inquiries is a rich, forward-looking volume that provides us with a first glimpse into the future of Indonesia in the post-Suharto era.

Lawrence J. Korb
Maurice R. Greenberg Chair, Director of Studies
Council on Foreign Relations

Prefatory Note

THIS book is the culmination of a Council on Foreign Relations Study Group on Indonesia that met in the first half of 1998, during one of the most tumultuous periods in Indonesian history. The study group was conceived well before the political upheaval in Indonesia and even before the Southeast Asian economic crisis began in the summer of 1997.

The motivating idea for organizing the study group was that while Suharto seemed firmly ensconced as Indonesia's president in 1997, the country was beginning an important transition period, which created uncertainty and fluidity in its political system, economic policies, social and ethnic relations, and foreign policy. We thought it critical for key opinion leaders to understand the forces and constituencies that would be likely to emerge and impact on the transition process to the next president, and begin to think through how the United States can deal with these forces and constituencies.

As became apparent when the economic crisis struck, there is considerable ignorance about Indonesia in nearly all branches of the U.S. government and in the business and academic communities. It seemed an opportune time, even without the intervening crisis, to focus on Indonesia. Indonesia is the fourth most populous country in the world. In addition to Indonesia's strategic importance, American investment in Indonesia has increased steadily since the beginning of the 1990s. Yet, unlike the northeast Asian powers—China, Japan, South Korea, and Taiwan—there does not exist, aside from lobby groups, an organized community of interests among the U.S. foreign policy elite that focuses on Indonesia.

The study group attempted to fill that gap by bringing together about 50 individuals drawn from the Council's membership and beyond, representing government, business, academia, the media, and nongovernmental organizations, to examine the coming changes in Indonesia.

This book is organized along the lines of the study group. The introduction by Adam Schwarz provides an overview covering the economic crisis, William Liddle's chapter analyzes Indonesian politics, Robert Hefner's chapter reviews Islam and ethnicity, Takashi Shiraishi's chapter examines the role of the military, and John Bresnan's concluding chapter evaluates U.S. policy toward Indonesia. The unifying theme of the chapters is an assessment of the forces and constituencies that are emerging in the transition to a post-Suharto Indonesia.

Schwarz's introduction provides some of the insights gained in the discussions at the five study group meetings, each of which took place while Indonesia was in a sharp crisis. The February session on the economy and religion/ethnicity occurred while the recently signed second International Monetary Fund agreement was unraveling, Suharto's selection of B. J. Habibie as vice president was provoking a free fall in the Indonesian rupiah, and Islamic-Christian and anti-Chinese tensions were rising. The second meeting on politics and the military took place in early April after the reelected Suharto named a number of family cronies to the cabinet and student demonstrators began confronting an indecisive army. The final session was held in Washington in May 1998, two weeks before the riots in Jakarta and Suharto's resignation.

The fortuitous timing of this project enabled the Council to produce one of the first books on Indonesia to come out since the end of the Suharto era. This book sheds light on a country in the middle of a devastating economic depression that is undergoing an important democratic transition filled with risks to the social fabric and opportunities for greater equality, fairness, and political participation. It is hoped that this volume will provide insights into Indonesia in the post-Suharto era and the challenges it poses for U.S. policy.

The Council Study Group on Indonesia that preceded this book was conceived following a visit I made to Jakarta as a member of a Council delegation in 1996. Prior to joining the Council on Foreign Relations as a Fellow, I had practiced law in Indonesia in the 1980s, and I remained keenly interested in developments in the country. The project crystallized when Adam Schwarz, a widely recognized Indonesian expert, became the Edward R. Murrow Fellow at the Council and joined me as codirector of the study group and coeditor of this book.

This study group would not have succeeded without the special role that John Bresnan played as chair and adviser. Three other outstanding international experts on Indonesia, Robert Hefner, William Liddle and Takashi Shiraishi, also contributed their time and talents to this book. We acknowledge the special contribution to the study group of several experts. Iwan Jaya Azia, professor at Cornell University, opened the study group with a presentation on the economic crisis. Serving as respondents for the other presentations were Colonel (ret.) John Haseman, former U.S.

Army defense attaché in Indonesia; Sidney Jones, executive director of Human Rights Watch/Asia; Dan Lev, professor at the University of Washington, and Saiful Mujani of Ohio State University.

This project was made possible by the financial support of GE Fund, Texaco, and other U.S. donors who remain anonymous. We acknowledge Les Gelb, president of the Council on Foreign Relations, for seeding the project with initial funding and for supporting the project before Indonesia became a headline story. Special thanks are due to Gary F. Hufbauer, whose tenure as director of studies at the Council on Foreign Relations coincided with the inception of the project. Gary provided intellectual, moral, and administrative support for this project throughout.

Jonathan Paris

1

Introduction: The Politics of Post-Suharto Indonesia

ADAM SCHWARZ

WHEN THE Indonesia Study Group of the Council on Foreign Relations first convened in early 1998, virtually all 50 members of the group prudently took the view that the post-Suharto era lay beyond the immediate horizon. Few predicted that the coming year would prove to be among the most tumultuous of Indonesia's history and bring an end to President Suharto's rule. As the year began, Suharto had been in office almost 32 years, and several months later he was dutifully sworn into office for another five-year term. Although the financial crisis sweeping Asia had already dealt a mortal blow to Indonesia's economic prospects, Suharto's hold on power appeared secure. As the months passed by, however, it became increasingly clear that the post-Suharto era stood a good chance of arriving sooner rather than later.

The fifth and final session of the study group met two weeks before Suharto, faced with sporadic urban violence and a steady succession of student-led demonstrations, resigned on May 21. The essays in this volume, updated through July, aim to shed light on the difficult and unpredictable task of political reform in Indonesia. Reflecting the discussions during the five study group sessions, the authors focus on the major themes of that reform process and the key actors who will lead it.

During his three decades of authoritarian rule, Suharto succeeded in restoring political stability to Indonesia and putting in place the policies that changed Indonesia from an economic basket case to a thriving, developmental success story. Average annual growth in excess of

7 percent led to a more than 10-fold rise in Indonesians' per capita income and a decline in the number of people in poverty from an estimated 70 percent of the population in the late 1960s to around 11 percent by the mid-1990s.

But Suharto's tightfisted control of the political system created its own set of problems. By muzzling the press and prohibiting free political competition, Suharto kept out of sight but did not eliminate a number of potentially divisive flash points within Indonesian society. These included relations between the country's many ethnic minorities, and in particular the ethnic distribution of economic wealth; the relationship between Islam—the religion of 88 percent of Indonesians—and the state; the military's role in politics; and the form of nationhood binding the outer islands to Java, where 60 percent of Indonesians live. As discussed elsewhere in this volume, all these issues came to the fore the day Suharto resigned. And as Indonesia moves forward in reconstructing its political architecture, these are the issues that lie at the heart of its political discourse.

The ethnic issue burst into the open even before Suharto left office. The violence that struck Jakarta in the second week of May was largely directed at the ethnic Chinese community. Comprising 4 percent of the population, the Chinese control up to 70 percent of the private, modern economy and are especially dominant in banking, trading, and distribution. Because of their economic dominance, the Chinese have long been resented by the country's indigenous majority, although they were rarely the targets of physical violence during Suharto's New Order regime. That changed with a vengeance in Suharto's last months in office.

In the last spasm of violence that preceded Suharto's resignation, Chinese neighborhoods in Jakarta were attacked by mobs, Chinese-owned shops were looted and burned, and most disturbing of all, scores of ethnic Chinese women were raped, many of them gang-raped, during three days of rioting. Many ethnic Chinese believe anti-Chinese officers in the military, led by Suharto's son-in-law Lieutenant-General Prabowo Subianto, incited the riots and were deliberately slow in putting a stop to them. Not surprisingly, the ethnic Chinese entered the post-Suharto era a traumatized community, unsure of its place in Indonesian society and fearful of its own security.

The fear felt by the Chinese resonated within Indonesia's other ethnic minorities, who wondered how they would be treated by the indigenous majority as Indonesia moved to a more democratic political system. In terms of assuring ethnic harmony, the post-Suharto era began on an inauspicious note.

Indonesian Islam is difficult to characterize. As William Liddle and Robert Hefner discuss in chapters 2 and 3, Indonesian Muslims form a pluralistic community. Many view their faith as a social and moral guide and are content to keep Islam largely separate from the state. Others believe that Islam properly understood does not permit such a separation; they insist that Indonesia's government be overtly Islamic.

As of this writing in August 1998, some 57 new political parties had been formed since President B. J. Habibie assumed office in the third week of May; a dozen were directly linked to Islamic groups. Which view of Islam will garner the most support in a fair election cannot be predicted. What can be said with more certainty is that a victory by the more strident voices in the Muslim community will pose a serious challenge to Indonesia's national integrity. Many of the outer, less-populated islands have large communities of Christians whose willingness to remain part of an Indonesia ruled by an overtly Islamic government is not assured. This same issue bedeviled Indonesia's founding fathers in the mid-1940s. It was resolved ultimately by a decision not to make Islam the basis of the state. Whether a democratic process a half century later will produce the same result remains unclear.

The Indonesian Armed Forces (ABRI) provided the backbone to Suharto's rule, both militarily and politically. Under its dual-function doctrine, ABRI took a direct role in day-to-day politics; military officers served in the cabinet, as governors and ambassadors, and were allocated reserved seats in the parliament. But with Suharto's departure, ABRI's political role is also being questioned. Many pro-reform activists are demanding ABRI's involvement in politics be severely curtailed, pointing to emerging evidence of widespread human rights violations not only in the run-up to Suharto's departure but also over a much longer period in places such as East Timor and Aceh.

At the other end of the political spectrum are voices demanding ABRI's dual-function role be maintained, at least for the foreseeable future. These voices argue that only ABRI can hold the nation together until the political system is reorganized. Some leaders of ethnic and religious minorities also see ABRI as the only institution capable of ensuring that minority rights are protected in a liberalized political system.

Suharto's Indonesia was a highly centralized operation. All political power resided in Jakarta, and with political power came control over the nation's economic wealth. With Suharto out of office, pressures for decentralization arose immediately. Advocates of decentralization argued on the grounds both of economic efficiency and of political expediency, noting the resentment generated in the outer islands at Jakarta's dominance.

But it is far from clear that decentralization will suffice for some of the more aggrieved areas furthest from Jakarta. Secessionist movements are active in East Timor, Aceh, and Irian Jaya. Jakarta is engaged in dialogue with Lisbon on the fate of East Timor, a former Portuguese colony. The Habibie administration has offered a form of autonomy to East Timor, while some activists in East Timor are demanding immediate independence. In Aceh, the discovery of mass graves containing bodies apparently of those killed by the Indonesian military in the early 1990s has revived secessionist sentiment. In Irian Jaya, rich in natural resources such as copper, gold, and oil, local community leaders are demanding a larger share of the wealth located in the province.

All these issues were discussed at length during the study group's five meetings and are explored in the essays that follow. Opinions diverged, naturally, on how each of these issues would be resolved and how they would impact the political liberalization process. Opinions also varied on the role played by international institutions and major world actors, especially the United States, in dealing with the financial crisis initially and on how they should assist Indonesia as it grapples with an economy bordering on collapse.

But there was general agreement that the current moment in Indonesia represents a historic turning point for the world's fourth most populous nation. As in 1945 when independence was proclaimed and in 1965–66 when President Sukarno, Indonesia's founding father, was replaced by then Major-General Suharto in a process that claimed several hundred thousand lives, the period 1998–99 is likely to determine Indonesia's future for many years to come.

Indonesia's rapid economic slide in the first half of 1998 provided the subplot for all the study group's sessions. The performance of Indonesia's economy in the 12 months beginning with August 1997 has been described as the most severe economic collapse suffered by any country since World War II. By the summer of 1998, the number of Indonesians living under the poverty line had risen from 20 million to 80 million and was headed higher. For the calendar year 1998, the economy was expected to contract by as much as 15 percent. Millions of workers were idled, inflation was heading up to triple digits, and the food distribution system was barely holding together.

For Suharto, who rested his claim to political power on his ability to sustain economic growth, the economic crisis deeply undermined his legitimacy and left him at last vulnerable to a credible challenge for power. But the economy had a bearing on all the major issues of the day. It influenced the thinking of indigenous Indonesian business leaders on how to reduce the economic dominance of the ethnic Chinese community; it sparked calls for greater decentralization on the part of resource-rich provinces; and it constrained the military's choices in the weeks and months leading up to Suharto's departure.

When the study group first met in February, Indonesia had already signed two reform packages with the International Monetary Fund (IMF). Indonesia floated its currency in August 1997, a month after Thailand had done the same. As with the Thai baht, the rupiah flotation only served to make matters worse. Instead of restoring confidence by improving export competitiveness, the weaker rupiah further undermined investor confidence by making it less likely Indonesia's highly indebted corporations would be able to repay their foreign currency borrowings.

Indonesia's private sector debt reached $80 billion, most of it unhedged. With a misplaced confidence in the central bank's ability to maintain in perpetuity a slow and steady depreciation of the rupiah against the U.S. dollar, Indonesian companies had borrowed heavily abroad to take advantage of lower interest rates. A significant part of the money was invested in unprofitable real estate or siphoned off by Indonesia's notoriously corrupt business elite, the most prominent members of which were the children and close relatives of President Suharto. As the rupiah began to slide in the summer of 1997, companies scrambled to buy dollars to pay off their debts, putting further downward pressure on the rupiah.

When the IMF was called in by Indonesia in October 1997, it negotiated a $43 billion bailout package intended to restore the confidence of foreign lenders and investors. Following its standard crisis-management menu, the IMF demanded a fiscal tightening that included the winding down of food subsidies, ordered the closing of 16 privately owned banks, and encouraged central bank officials to raise interest rates in what turned out to be an unsuccessful attempt to make the rupiah more attractive to offshore investors.

As John Bresnan points out in chapter 5, the first IMF agreement was attacked for both doing too much and doing too little. The closing of the 16 banks accomplished little more than setting off a run on the rest of Indonesia's banks. Without any form of deposit insurance or any idea whether more banks had been ordered closed by the IMF, Indonesian depositors did the prudent thing and withdrew their savings. The effect was to take billions of rupiah out of circulation and further restrict banks' ability to lend. Study group participants also criticized the IMF for insisting on a fiscal tightening when the government had not previously been running a budget deficit; cutting government spending merely exacerbated the deflationary pressures on the private sector.

At the same time, critics assailed the IMF for not doing more to attack the roots of Suharto's patronage network and to insist on an end to the more obvious cases of favoritism shown Suharto's children and cronies. This argument gained currency when Suharto's middle son, Bambang Trihatmodjo, who owned one of the 16 closed banks, was able to reopen his bank under a new name only a week later.

Indonesia's economy continued to decline in the last months of 1997 and then headed sharply lower in the first week of January when Suharto announced a budget that was considered wildly optimistic by many observers. Investors concluded that Suharto still did not appreciate the dimensions of the crisis afflicting Indonesia's economy and continued to dump the rupiah.

On January 15, 1998, Indonesia and the IMF signed a second, much more comprehensive agreement. The second agreement stipulated specific measures to cut subsidies across the board and ordered an end to numerous market-distorting cartels and monopolies, all of which benefited Suharto's friends and family. Among the most politically sensitive of the measures was an end to government funding for the state-owned aircraft-manufacturing operation then headed by B. J. Habibie, the current president; the scrapping of tax breaks awarded to a national car project headed by Suharto's youngest son, Hutomo Mandala Putra; and an end to the plywood cartel controled by Suharto's long-standing confidant Mohammad "Bob" Hasan.

Like the first IMF agreement, however, the second deal barely made a dent in the market psyche. Although it contained many measures investors had been clamoring for, its effectiveness was fatally undermined by two events. The first was a string of riots in mostly small towns in Java that targeted ethnic-Chinese–owned businesses and shops. The attacks on the Chinese disrupted the food distribution system and paved the way for further unrest. In addition, they discouraged wealthier Chinese-owned businesses in the major cities from repatriating funds from overseas.

The second event was the indication in mid-January that Suharto intended to choose Research and Technology Minister B. J. Habibie as his next vice president for the term scheduled to begin in March 1998. Habibie was well known as a proponent of massive state subsidies for high-technology industries, all of which have been carefully shielded from public accounting. He was also considered an opponent of the technocrats in the Finance Ministry who were the primary interlocutors of the IMF. The belief that Habibie was Suharto's choice for the vice presidency convinced investors that Suharto was not up to the task of implementing the reforms he had agreed to with the IMF and that he had lost faith in his economic ministers. The rupiah dropped to as low as 17,000 against the U.S. dollar, compared with 2,500 just seven months earlier.

This was the backdrop to the study group's first meeting in early February. Participants discussed the causes of Indonesia's economic crisis and the merits of Suharto's short-lived plan to impose a currency board as a means for lowering the rupiah-dollar exchange rate. But the bulk of the discussion centered on the performance of the IMF. As discussed above, study group participants were almost unanimously critical of the IMF's initial attempts at financial sector reform as well as its insistence that Jakarta sharply reduce food and fuel subsidies.

Another area of criticism centered on the January 15, 1998, package, in which the IMF mandated sweeping liberalization measures in a number of politically sensitive areas. Cornell University economist Iwan Jaya Aziz, among others, accused the IMF of overreaching its mandate by focusing on high-profile arrangements favorable to Suharto's children and close friends. These critics contended that requiring the closure of a clove-trading monopoly controlled by Suharto's youngest son, to take one example, may have been satisfying in a public relations sense, but did not address the core reasons behind the rupiah's weakness. Others argued that the IMF's approach was doomed to fail because it insisted on measures that would weaken Suharto politically and that therefore would be resisted by the Indonesian president.

But the majority of the study group felt, as John Bresnan writes, that the IMF had little choice but to take the approach it did. The IMF's fundamental goal was to restore confidence in the Indonesian economy, in the eyes of both domestic and foreign investors. Given the debacle following the first IMF package in October 1997, the IMF concluded that the only way to restore confidence was to show that Suharto was serious about economic reform, a process that necessarily involved a new, more transparent relationship between the government and the private business sector. The IMF's view, shared by most study group participants, was that the only way for Suharto to convince an increasingly skeptical market that he was committed to fundamental reform was to put an end to some of the more egregious market-distorting practices that had enriched his inner circle.

In the study group session focusing on politics, William Liddle discussed Suharto's strangely detached response to the financial crisis. In the past, Suharto had been known for acting decisively on economic problems. Following the Pertamina debt scandal in the mid-1970s, for example, or the collapse in oil prices in the mid-1980s, Suharto handed the reins of economic policy to his team of technocrats at the Finance Ministry, who proceeded to implement successfully a series of market reforms. In the summer of 1997, many international observers felt Indonesia would weather the economic storm passing through Asia relatively well, partly on account of Suharto's impressive record of crisis management.

What changed in 1998? In Liddle's view, the answer is two fold. On the one hand, the reforms required of Suharto in the latest crisis infringed on his power and his patronage networks far more intrusively than in previous crises. Unlike in the past, in the crisis of 1997–98 Suharto was ultimately unable to reconcile the demands for economic reform with his own political prerogatives.

But a second reason is more personal than political. When the latest financial crisis began, Suharto was 76 years old. As Liddle points out, he had grown increasingly isolated and aloof from the political process. He had come to depend on the advice and counsel of his family and business cronies. When the crisis emerged, Suharto was in relatively short order pushed to choose between the interests of the nation and the interests of his family and friends. He opted for the latter, with tragic consequences for both himself and the nation.

Observers of Indonesian politics have little to go on in trying to predict the future course of events. Political loyalties have been submerged for over four decades, first under the increasingly authoritarian policies of Indonesia's founding father, Sukarno, and then under Suharto. The last, and only, free elections in Indonesia's history took place in 1955. Liddle argues that the results of the 1955 elections provide a rough blueprint for the elections scheduled for 1999.

The four major parties active in the 1950s collected 80 percent of the vote in the 1955 elections. They included the Nationalist Party, PNI, which attracted middle- and upper-class groups; the Communist Party, PKI, which was supported by urban workers and landless farmers; the modernist Muslim grouping, Masjumi; and the Nahdlatul Ulama (NU), which was the political vehicle of traditionalist Muslims.

Of the four, only the NU remains intact in the 1990s, although since the mid-1980s it has not considered itself a political organization. However, the religious and class differences that distinguished the four main parties in the 1950s still exist and, Liddle argues, are likely to make themselves felt in Indonesia's next elections. The secular, nationalist forces that once supported the PNI, for example, are expected to gravitate to new offshoots of Golkar, Suharto's political party, or to the Indonesian Democratic Party, the most popular faction of which is now led by Sukarno's daughter Megawati Sukarnoputri.

Likewise, the rural peasantry and urban underclass that once supported the Communist Party are likely to vote for newly established parties that represent farmer and labor interests. The modernist Muslims that were earlier grouped under the Masjumi have an expanding choice of Islamic parties to support, the largest of which is linked to the Muhammadiyah, a 28-million strong Islamic organization that is second in size only to the NU.

To be sure, new actors have emerged in the more than 40 years since the 1955 elections. Liddle cites the indigenous Indonesian business class as one group to watch. Sidney Jones, executive director of Human Rights Watch/Asia, noted the increasingly important role played by student groups and nongovernmental organizations in the process leading up to Suharto's downfall. She suggested these groups would continue to have an important, if difficult to predict, influence on the politics of post-Suharto Indonesia. Both Liddle and Jones pointed out that Java's dominance of the political process was likely to decline in a more democratic Indonesia, mostly on account of strong pressures for a more decentralized management of the economy.

Looking forward, Liddle notes that President Habibie faces enormous challenges on every front. He must contend with widespread economic devastation and resolve the stifling corporate debt problem. He needs to reassure ethnic-Chinese Indonesians that their physical and material security is assured in a more democratic Indonesia. He must walk a fine line between pro-reform activists pushing for immediate liberalization and a nervous military concerned about national stability. He must balance the demand for democratic politics with the need to protect the rights of minorities. He must oversee a difficult transition to free elections that will produce a leader with a genuine mandate from the Indonesian people. And he must accomplish all this even though, as Liddle writes, his "personal support remains weak, and his coalition is fragile." The road to a democratic Indonesia is not likely to be smooth.

The political views of Indonesia's Muslim majority represent perhaps the greatest uncertainty in the current political transition. As Robert Hefner discussed in the study group's session on Islam and ethnicity, there is no single Muslim voice in Indonesia. There are, rather, a number of competing visions of Islam; which one will prevail in the political contests of the future is hard to predict.

Historians and anthropologists commonly divide Indonesia's Muslim community into two broad groupings. Traditionalist Muslims are generally found in the rural, less-affluent parts of the country, especially Java. They hew to a syncretic view of Islam that incorporates some of the cultural traditions that predated Islam's arrival in the Indonesian archipelago. They are relatively tolerant of different professions of the Islamic faith; politically, as Hefner writes, they are "imbued with populist or progressive nationalist sentiments." The 30-million strong NU, led by Abdurrahman Wahid, is the main traditionalist Islamic organization.

Modernist Muslims follow a more literal interpretation of the Koran. They have a broader national base than the traditionalists and are generally more urban, wealthy and formally educated. The more militant wing of the modernist community has objected since independence to the secular approach followed by the country's leadership, including the military. The mainstream Muhammadiyah, led by Amien Rais, is the largest modernist grouping.

In the last years of his rule, Suharto reached out to the modernists by endorsing the formation of the Indonesian Association of Muslim Intellectuals (ICMI), a collection of mostly modernist intellectuals and civil service bureaucrats close to Suharto. Headed until recently by the current president, B. J. Habibie, ICMI has been vigorously criticized by some traditionalist leaders.

Many Indonesians fall into the category of nominal, or *abangan,* Muslims. While they may follow Islamic customs and practices in their private lives, they do not support an overtly Islamic presence in government. Generally speaking, they are unlikely to support political parties with a specifically Islamic agenda. On the other end of the spectrum are small groups of militant Islamic activists, many of whom desire Indonesia to adopt Islam as the fundamental basis of the state. These groups tend to be strongly anti-Chinese and anti-Christian and follow a generally anti-Western line in foreign policy.

In all these groups, contradictions abound. The NU's leader Abdurrahman Wahid is a worldly, sophisticated intellectual who has long championed democratic ideals. Yet members of the NU have on occasion participated in acts of religious and racial intolerance. In 1996, for example, anti-Chinese and anti-Christian riots broke out in the East Java city of Situbondo, an NU stronghold. (Some NU leaders, as Hefner reports, claim the riots were instigated by outside forces, possibly linked to ICMI or the military, in an attempt to discredit Wahid.) More recently, NU supporters have blocked the Muhammadiyah leader Amien Rais from speaking at political rallies in East Java.

Modernist Muslims, on the other hand, have been frequent targets of criticism by nominal Muslims and non-Muslims for being religiously intolerant and antidemocratic. Yet modernist groups played a key role in the pro-reform coalition that succeeded in forcing Suharto from power.

The Muhammadiyah leader Amien Rais has been one of the most articulate voices calling for democratic governance and ethnic tolerance.

As Indonesia becomes more democratic, there is little doubt that Islam will come to have a greater role in the formal political sphere. What that role will be is uncertain, although there are solid grounds for believing Islam and democracy can and will coexist harmoniously. As Hefner writes, "Nowhere in the Muslim world have Muslim intellectuals engaged the ideas of democracy, civil society, pluralism, and the rule of law with a vigor and confidence equal to that of Indonesian Muslims."

Still, a number of possible roadblocks lies ahead. One is the ongoing economic crisis, which has tended to aggravate relations between parts of the Muslim community and the mostly Christian ethnic-Chinese minority. Another is the attitude taken by political elites and the possible ways in which they may appeal to specifically Muslim grievances in a bid to generate electoral support.

A third is the approach taken by the military in accommodating a greater political role for Islam. How will it reconcile its secular traditions with an Islamic political revival? Finally, as the Ohio State University scholar Saiful Mujani points out, caution is needed in assessing the political inclinations of Indonesia's Muslims. For over four decades, Indonesian Muslims have not been free to express their views on the proper relationship between Islam and the state. Past public statements by Muslim leaders and the formal positions of Islamic groups need therefore to be taken with a grain of salt. Mujani argues that only after a free and fair democratic process can the true views of Indonesia's Muslims be discerned.

Indonesia's military has been at the center of the nation's political life since independence was proclaimed in 1945. In its own view of the 1950s, the military, known by the acronym ABRI, saved the nation from fickle and incompetent civilian politicians time after time. ABRI began to develop its dual-function doctrine in the late 1950s and expanded it significantly under Suharto's New Order government.

As described earlier, ABRI's dual-function doctrine entitled the military to a major political role via assignments to governorships, cabinet positions, and parliamentary seats. But as Takashi Shiraishi writes, ABRI's political clout has been in decline for most of the 1990s.

The study group session on the Indonesian military noted that ABRI's weakening political standing occurred as Suharto's strengthened. Having overcome all challenges to his rule, by the late 1980s Suharto no longer required a politically strong military and could afford to let ABRI's political power decline. In addition, Suharto's animosity toward former armed forces commander General Benny Murdani resulted in a sweeping reorganization of the military's intelligence operations, which had been Murdani's principal power base. The effect was to weaken ABRI's capacity to anticipate and react to political events. Finally, in the early 1990s Suharto began to shuffle officers rapidly through senior command and staff posts, which made it difficult for up-and-coming officers to develop their own core of supporters.

Meanwhile, reflecting Suharto's own manipulation of the Islamic community, ABRI began to develop a schism along religious lines. The so-called red-and-white faction represented the military's nationalist, secular wing. Its leader in the period leading up to Suharto's resignation was the current armed forces commander, General Wiranto. A green faction was composed of officers known to be close to modernist Muslims; its leader until May 1998 was Suharto's son-in-law Lieutenant-General Prabowo Subianto.

It is not clear how deep or tightly drawn these divisions were. But on the basis of the evidence currently available, it seems they were deep enough to render the military politically ineffectual during the last months of Suharto's rule. As Shiraishi points out, for the military to take a political stance independent of Suharto, its top leaders would have to agree on a course of action. The alternative was to risk a civil war, an outcome neither side desired.

By ensuring that both Wiranto and Prabowo had important allies in key military commands, Suharto made it all but impossible for the military to reach any sort of consensus independent of Suharto's wishes. Even during the last weeks and months of Suharto's rule, the military remained divided on how to respond to street-level demonstrations and unable to muster a single voice with which to communicate with Suharto.

Immediately following Suharto's resignation, Wiranto moved to consolidate control of the military. He dismissed Prabowo from the command of the Army Strategic Reserve, and subsequently dismissed or removed from troop command a number of Prabowo's key allies.

But although military unity has been at least partially restored, ABRI remains a weakened political actor. The alleged involvement of Prabowo and his allies in the abduction and torture of democracy activists, in the shooting of unarmed civilians in Jakarta in May 1998, and in the instigation of riots that rocked Jakarta just before Suharto resigned, have badly besmirched ABRI's reputation and called into question its right to a prominent political role.

Wiranto ordered a military investigation of Prabowo and his allies, which at the time of this writing had yet to run its course. But even if the military perpetrators of the criminal activities listed above are brought to justice, ABRI faces a long road ahead in restoring its credibility in the eyes of the Indonesian people. Information is already coming to light on ABRI atrocities committed in Aceh, East Timor, and Irian Jaya, further tarnishing ABRI's reputation.

In addition, ABRI has not been immune to the economic crisis. Funding shortages have forced ABRI to shrink its forces and cut already meager wages to its troops. John Haseman, a former U.S. defense attaché in Jakarta, noted that ABRI's procurement of military equipment has dropped to practically zero in the past two years.

Despite all these setbacks, Indonesia's military remains the preeminent political institution in the country, almost by default. Suharto's efforts at depoliticizing Indonesia were so successful that when he left office, the military was the only functioning political institution left standing. The task ahead for ABRI is to redefine its dual-function doctrine to match the political liberalization process now under way. ABRI's security approach, which relied all too often on repression and force, needs to give way to an approach based more on negotiation and dialogue.

At the same time, Shiraishi points out that ABRI has no intention of returning immediately to the barracks, an outcome that is being demanded by some of the more militant pro-reform groups. ABRI sees itself as the only force capable of ensuring that civilian politicians do not use their newly won freedoms to stir up old ethnic and religious antagonisms and thereby threaten national unity. A number of senior officers are known to be uncomfortable with President Habibie's freeing of political prisoners and his willingness to grant significant autonomy to East Timor. As Liddle and others point out, it is not inconceivable that the military would retake control of the government if it feels the civilian political elites are threatening the nation's territorial integrity and social stability.

The most contentious of the study group's sessions was its final meeting, which looked at U.S. policy toward Indonesia since the beginning of the economic crisis. The American failure to participate directly in the IMF-brokered, $17 billion bailout package for Thailand in August 1997 was widely criticized by U.S. allies in Asia. The United States did participate in the IMF's $43 billion package for Indonesia, announced in October 1997, pledging $3 billion to the so-called second line of defense.

As the IMF began to broaden its reform demands on Indonesia, the United States, as the IMF's largest shareholder, was gradually drawn into the political drama being played out in Jakarta. President Clinton, concerned about the contagion effect on other emerging markets, made a series of telephone calls to Suharto in early 1998, encouraging him to abide by the agreements he had signed with the IMF. Clinton later sent former vice president Walter Mondale to Jakarta as his personal emissary to deliver the same message. John Bresnan writes that this activity constituted the greatest U.S. intervention in Indonesian affairs since President Lyndon Johnson sent Attorney General Robert Kennedy to Jakarta in the mid-1960s to convince President Sukarno to call off the *konfrontasi* with Malaysia.

Bresnan was critical of the U.S. response to the Indonesian crisis, saying a lack of coordination by the White House and an administration-wide shortage of Indonesian expertise resulted in confusing and at times contradictory messages being sent by Washington. The U.S. military, he added, failed to respond to widespread allegations of human rights abuses committed by the Special Forces (Kopassus) unit headed until early 1998 by Lieutenant-General Prabowo Subianto. A number of senior Kopassus officers, including Prabowo, had been trained in the United States under the International Military Education and Training program (IMET), and U.S. military units had conducted a series of joint exercises and training missions with Kopassus forces.

At a broader level, Bresnan criticized the Clinton administration for failing to develop an overall strategy for coping with the Asian crisis. He said this was due to a number of reasons, among them the White House's caution in helping Indonesia, given Clinton's controversial fund-raising overtures to Indonesian businessmen; the White House's preoccupation with the investigation of Independent Counsel Kenneth Starr; and the fact that the Asian financial crisis had not materially affected the American economy.

Bresnan commended the administration for resisting calls from Congress to demand Suharto's resignation in the weeks prior to his standing down. Looking forward, Bresnan said the top U.S. priority must be to help relieve the suffering of the Indonesian people and called for generous humanitarian assistance. The United States has a major stake in Indonesia's experiment with political reform, he concluded, but noted that the United States would have little leverage to influence developments in Indonesia if it stood by while the Indonesian economy crumbled. Bresnan also said the United States would be well served by turning a sympathetic ear to calls by developing countries for constructing some safeguards against the ravaging effects of highly volatile, short-term capital flows.

Dan Lev, a political scientist from the University of Washington, took a more critical view of the U.S. approach to Indonesia. He argued that Suharto's authoritarianism was the principal cause of Indonesia's economic troubles. As such, he said, only fundamental political change could solve Indonesia's crisis. If the Clinton administration was unwilling to push for Suharto's removal, it ought not to have participated in the various IMF rescue packages that, Lev said, were doomed to failure. He agreed with Bresnan that the United States should cut off all training and cooperation programs with the Indonesian military.

A large majority of the study group participants disagreed with Lev's analysis. The general feeling was that Washington had little choice but to participate in the IMF rescue packages for Indonesia or put at risk its long-term political and security interests in Indonesia and elsewhere in Asia. Most participants felt the United States was right to support the IMF's demand for comprehensive structural reform in Indonesia, even at the risk of courting Suharto's ire. To do otherwise, they felt, would have succeeded only in wasting the international bailout funds, failing to restore international confidence in Indonesia, and weakening U.S. congressional support for the IMF.

Finally, a number of participants defended U.S. military cooperation with the Indonesian armed forces. They argued that the IMET program was useful in exposing promising Indonesian officers to the nature of civilian-military relations in a democracy. It also provided the United States with useful contacts inside the Indonesian military. They contended that the U.S. military training programs with Indonesia should not be sacrificed because of the actions, admittedly deplorable, of a few U.S.-trained officers. One Indonesian participant in the study group who supports the IMET program put it this way: "Jesus only had to pick 12 disciples, and even he picked one bad apple."

2

Indonesia's Unexpected Failure of Leadership

R. WILLIAM LIDDLE

We are very worried. He is making the wrong decisions but nobody can oppose him. He is all-powerful and we are dependent on his leadership.[1]

Sebuah negeri yang diperintah oleh satu orang bukanlah sebuah negeri sama sekali. *[A country that is governed by one person is not a country at all.]*[2]

The Present

On May 21, 1998, in a brief ceremony broadcast around the world, Indonesia's President Suharto resigned and was replaced by his vice president of only two months, B. J. Habibie, a Suharto confidant who had served for many years as minister of research and technology. Suharto had held power for more than 32 years, and until his final days in office few observers predicted that the end was near.

Suharto's decision to resign was precipitated by the refusal of 14 key individuals, led by Coordinating Minister for the Economy, Finance, and Industry Ginandjar Kartasasmita, to accept appointment as ministers in a restructured cabinet. He was also under severe pressure to step down from the leaders of the People's Consultative Assembly (Majelis Permusyawaratan Rakyat), the superparliamentary constitutional body that in March had elected him president for his seventh five-year term. These events took place in a context of economic and political turmoil that began with the July 1997 currency crisis. It included massive student demonstrations at university campuses across the country beginning the following February; the murder, allegedly by security forces, of four students at a private Jakarta university on May 12; an orgy of urban rioting during May 13–15 that claimed more than 1,000 lives; and the seizure of the Assembly building on May 18 by several thousand students. It was this last event that drove the Assembly leaders, all previously handpicked by Suharto himself, to turn against their boss, and the president's abortive cabinet restructuring was his initial response to it.

How can we explain Suharto's rapid political demise, after so many years of near-absolute power? Age—Suharto turned 77 in June 1998—was undoubtedly a factor, as was the depth of the economic crisis, the most serious that Indonesia has experienced since the beginning of the New Order government established by Suharto in 1965–66. More important, however, was a series of presidential policy missteps that worsened and prolonged the crisis. While other East and Southeast Asian economies, particularly those of Thailand and South Korea, appeared by the early part of 1998 to have turned a corner toward renewed prosperity, the Indonesian decline continued. In March 1998, when Suharto's worst political troubles began, the rupiah was trading at above 10,000 to the U.S. dollar (for those few willing to buy it); most banks and many modern sector businesses were technically bankrupt if not actually shut down; millions of people had lost their jobs; inflation was running at an annual rate of 150 percent; and there were shortages of basic commodities, including medical supplies as well as foodstuffs and other common household items.

The International Monetary Fund (IMF), backed by the World Bank and the governments of the G-7 countries, had twice—in October 1997 and January 1998—offered to bail Suharto out by providing new credits in return for economic reforms. On both occasions the president formally accepted the Fund's terms but almost immediately proceeded to subvert the agreement in ways too obvious for foreign financial markets and investors to miss. For example, after the first agreement the bank of his son Bambang Trihatmodjo was closed as stipulated, but its assets were placed in another Bambang-owned bank. Construction of a Suharto-linked hydroelectric project in East Java was first postponed, then rescheduled. In early January, an overly optimistic 1998–99 state budget was announced without prior consultation with the Fund.

The second, much more sweeping and more stringent agreement, subsequently known as the IMF's 50-point program, was signed on January 15, 1998. Within weeks there were reports that this agreement was being breached as well. For example, ways were found to maintain both the clove monopoly and the national car project controlled by youngest son Tommy (Hutomo Mandala Putra). Presidential crony Mohammad "Bob" Hasan moved quickly to reestablish his tight grip on the plywood industry. The construction company owned by oldest daughter Tutut (Siti Hardiyanti Rukmana) announced that it would still build an expensive triple-decker road.

During this same period Suharto also took, or allowed others to take, actions that distracted attention from the real causes of and possible solutions to the economic crisis. For example, daughter Tutut played a key role in the Love the Rupiah Movement, in which middle- and upper-class Indonesians (Sino-Indonesians felt especially pressured) were urged to sell their dollars to help raise the value of the rupiah. A campaign was begun against the wealthiest Sino-Indonesian businesspeople (the so-called *konglomerat*), who were alleged to have parked tens of billions of dollars abroad.[3] The *konglomerat* were labeled unpatriotic by Armed Forces Commander General Feisal Tanjung, who threatened (although he did not carry out) "further action" if their capital was not returned to Indonesia and given to the state. One prominent Sino-Indonesian businessman, Sofyan Wanandi, was called in for questioning in connection with a bomb blast in a Jakarta apartment complex. The government's targeting of Sofyan was probably unrelated to the capital flight issue, but it further frightened the Sino-Indonesian business community.

The most distracting issue, which was debated in and outside Indonesia for nearly two months, was the proposal to peg the rupiah at approximately 5,000 to the U.S. dollar via a currency board. This idea was apparently initiated by a businessman close to the Suharto children, who invited currency board expert (and promoter) Professor Steven Hanke of Johns Hopkins University to the presidential residence. The currency board would have replaced the functions of the central bank by limiting the number of rupiah in circulation to the number of dollars available to redeem them at the fixed rate and by allowing bank interest rates to be set by the market. While most economists and businesspeople, domestic and foreign, quickly agreed that Indonesia was not a suitable candidate for a currency board (too few available dollars and too weak a banking system), the president was unwilling to abandon it.

This put him at odds with his own economic advisers, prompting him to fire the respected head of the central bank, Soedradjad Djiwandono. It also strained relations with the IMF, the World Bank, and G-7 governments, all of which wanted him to comply with the 50-point IMF program. Several telephone calls from U.S. President Bill Clinton, plus a steady stream of prominent visitors, including former U.S. Vice President

Walter Mondale and then Japanese Prime Minister Ryutaro Hashimoto, failed to change his mind. The break finally came on March 20, when newly appointed Finance Minister Fuad Bawazier, after meeting with a new IMF team, announced that the currency board idea would not be implemented because of the insufficiency of foreign reserves.[4]

During this same period, January–March, President Suharto made political decisions—particularly his choice of a vice president and cabinet—that increased doubts about his commitment to the 50-point IMF program. Under the constitution of 1945, the People's Consultative Assembly meets quinquennially to elect the president and vice president and to promulgate the "main outlines of state policy." According to New Order practice, soon after each Assembly session, the president appointed a new cabinet. Following this schedule, the Assembly met from March 1 to March 11, 1998, and the new cabinet, whose members were expected to serve until 2003, was announced on March 14.

The Assembly convened on March 1 consisted of the 425 elected and 75 appointed members of Parliament (Dewan Perwakilan Rakyat [DPR], or People's Representative Council) plus 500 appointed members. As in previous years, both the election and the appointment processes were closely managed by the president and his aides to ensure a minimum of opposition to Suharto's own reelection, his choice of a vice president, and his version of the outline of state policy. There has been a general election prior to every Assembly session (the last was held on May 29, 1997), at which three parties—one government and two nongovernment—were permitted to compete for the 425 seats. The government party, called Golkar (Golongan Karya, Functional Groups) is the partisan political face of the state bureaucracy and the military. It was first mobilized by Suharto prior to the parliamentary election of 1971 to minimize the role of nonstate political forces in Parliament and the Consultative Assembly.

The two nongovernment parties are themselves the product of a 1973 forced fusion by Suharto of nine previously autonomous parties. Throughout the New Order, they received stipends from a Suharto-controlled foundation, their leaders were approved by the government, and their campaign activities were limited and closely watched by the army. In June 1996 the popular Megawati Sukarnoputri, a daughter of the late President Sukarno (and for that reason potentially charismatic), was forcibly ousted as leader of the nationalist Christian Indonesian Democratic Party (Partai Demokrasi Indonesia, PDI) on Suharto's orders. The current leaders of the other nongovernment party, the Islamic PPP (Partai Persatuan Pembangunan, United Development Party), were not perceived to threaten the government.

In the 1997 parliamentary election Golkar won 325 seats, PPP 89, and PDI 11 (few PDI supporters were willing to vote for the party after Megawati's ouster). The Assembly that met in March 1998 consisted of these 425 representatives plus 75 armed forces appointees and 500 appointees, representing the regions, the parties, the armed forces, and a variety of otherwise unrepresented social groups. These appointments were all made in processes controlled by Suharto and therefore produced an Assembly prepared to do the president's bidding. His wishes included his own reelection and the election of his chosen vice president, former minister of research and technology B. J. Habibie, both by acclamation, plus the promulgation of an Assembly decision granting the president extraordinary powers in the event of a threat to national security.

The choice of Habibie did nothing to reassure the financial markets or potential investors in the Indonesian economy. Indeed, the immediate effect was to push the rupiah to a new low against the dollar. Habibie is a German-trained aeronautical engineer with a reputation for economic ignorance and little patience with anyone who disagrees with him. In his vision, as expressed in the 25 years he served Suharto, reliance on high-technology manufacturing by state industries will enable Indonesia to develop rapidly, leapfrogging countries that follow a conventional conception of comparative advantage. Well over a billion dollars in state funds were poured into Industri Pesawat Terbang Nusantara (IPTN), the state aircraft manufacturing company that he long headed. Although the company's books are not available for independent inspection, IPTN appears to have provided few returns on this enormous investment. Habibie also personally headed several other state companies and oversaw 10 so-called strategic industries. His person and policies have been anathema not only to the professional economists, the IMF, and so on, but also to many officers in the Indonesian armed forces. Habibie's control over the state shipbuilding and ammunition industries and his purchase a few years ago of the former East German Navy were viewed by many officers as direct threats to armed forces interests.

Suharto's choice of Habibie was probably planned long before, even as early as March 1993, when the president reluctantly accepted General Try Sutrisno, the nominee pressed on him by the armed forces, as his vice president for the 1993–98 term.[5] How Suharto intended to use Habibie in his new post is not clear. Habibie's assistants and associates reported that Habibie himself believed he had been designated Suharto's successor.[6] Many others, outside as well as inside the Habibie camp, argued that Habibie would be a kind of de facto prime minister, as an aging President

Suharto lost interest in the details of day-to-day policymaking. My own view is that Suharto did not intend to give his new vice president a role substantially greater than that assigned to his predecessors, nor did he expect to be succeeded by Habibie. On May 19, two days before he resigned, Suharto, still the master of indirect speech, told the press: "For me, resigning or not is not a problem. What we must think about is whether with my resignation the situation can quickly be overcome."[7]

The litmus test for membership in Suharto's new cabinet, particularly for the economic portfolios, appears to have been hostility to the IMF and willingness to accept a currency board. The new coordinating minister for the economy, finance, and industry, and simultaneously chair of the National Development Planning Board, Ginandjar Kartasasmita, was a presidential favorite long associated with protectionist policies for national entrepreneurs. The finance minister, Fuad Bawazier, was reported to be close to the Suharto children, while the new central bank governor, Sjahril Sabirin, was plucked from the relative obscurity of a World Bank staff position in Washington. Perhaps most revealing of Suharto's attitude toward the IMF was his startling appointment of plywood monopolist Bob Hasan as minister of trade and industry. The message appeared to be: "Not only will I not dismantle the cartels, but you will now have to negotiate directly with the cartel king!"

Unquestioned loyalty to Suharto clearly counted highly in the president's choices of many of the new ministers. This is consistent with his historic pattern of relations with the armed forces as well. Since 1988, when he dismissed General Benny Murdani as armed forces commander, and especially since 1993, when he appointed General Feisal Tanjung commander, Suharto went to great lengths to make sure that personal loyalists (mostly former adjutants and presidential guard commanders) were given all key command positions.[8] Finally, presidential first daughter Tutut appears to have been influential in the selection of several new cabinet members. The Singapore *Straits Times* reported that up to half the new ministers were her associates. Tutut herself, as minister for social affairs, became the first Suharto child to be given a cabinet post.

By mid-March, Suharto was standing in a deep hole that he himself had dug. The economic situation had worsened steadily, at least in part as a result of his own actions. A large proportion of the wage-earning working class and of the clerical, professional, and entrepreneurial middle and upper classes—inside as well as outside the government—had reluctantly come to see him as part of the problem. University students, the children of the middle and upper classes, were frightened by the sudden collapse of the economy and angry with the leader they believed responsible for their situation. They also had little to lose and potentially much to gain by mobilizing against the government. Moreover, with his vice presidential and cabinet appointments, Suharto had opened himself wide to charges of cronyism and nepotism.

At this point, Suharto's only important supporter was the armed forces, the main pillar on which he had constructed the New Order more than 30 years before. For weeks, the military under the leadership of newly appointed Armed Forces Commander General Wiranto, a former presidential adjutant, successfully kept the students contained behind the walls of their campuses, although popular support for their movement, especially among urban professionals, grew rapidly. The dam burst when four students at Trisakti University, a private university in Jakarta, were shot to death on May 12, allegedly by police who disobeyed instructions to use only rubber bullets. The funerals of the martyred students, carried live on national television, produced a new wave of protest, followed by the mass violence of May 13–15. Top military leaders finally realized that Suharto had to go and began to discuss possible scenarios. By this time, however, events were moving quickly, and the generals acted on their own less than they reacted to the moves of others, like the Assembly leaders and Economics Minister Ginandjar. Armed forces loyalty to Suharto as a person, if no longer as president, was evident at the resignation ceremony. Wiranto appealed to the nation to support the transition and added that "the armed forces will continue to protect the safety and the honor of former presidents . . . including Father Suharto and his family."[9]

The Past (Briefly Described)

To an observer of the New Order since its inception, the pattern of President Suharto's economic policy decisions from July 1997 until his resignation in May 1998 was strikingly aberrant. In the mid-1960s, when Suharto first took power from President Sukarno, the economy was in deep crisis, with a huge unpayable debt (at that time state, not private) to foreign creditors, nonfunctioning banks, a negative growth rate, and runaway inflation. At that time, the new president took the advice of his team of professional economists, the so-called Berkeley Mafia under the leadership of Professor Wijoyo Nitisastro, who were working closely with the IMF, World Bank, and other foreign lenders. Under the guidance of the Wijoyo team, and with new foreign credits, the economy quickly stabilized and then began to grow at a respectable rate, which soon averaged about 8 percent per year.

From the late 1960s to the early 1990s, a series of further crises shook the Indonesian economy, including the rice price crisis of 1973, the state oil company Pertamina's debt crisis in 1975, the world recession of 1981–82, and the collapse of the international petroleum price in 1986.[10] On each of these occasions, after a certain, but brief, hesitation, Suharto chose once again to follow the advice of the economists, which included the continuation of conservative macroeconomic policies and balanced budgets, plus new trade and (after 1988) financial liberalization. The result was restored growth, which in the 1990s has averaged about 7 percent.

This is not to suggest that the economists had no competition for Suharto's ear. Both Ginandjar, representing private indigenous business, and Habibie, representing high-technology state enterprise, have been major players for decades. Before them, the long-term Pertamina director, Ibnu Sutowo, borrowed (with Suharto's approval but without the knowledge of the economics ministers) billions of dollars to finance his own version of high-tech industries, such as floating rice estates. Indeed, Ginandjar, Habibie, and Sutowo all received favorable mention—Ginandjar and Habibie are singled out as particularly promising young officials—in Suharto's autobiography, while the names of Wijoyo and his team of economists do not appear at all.[11]

One conclusion that can be drawn from Suharto's autobiography is that he never felt warmly toward the economists but saw them instead as a necessary evil enabling him to extract from the international economy the resources he needed to develop Indonesia. It is also certainly true that he never shared their vision of an essentially free market economy. (In an American context, the Indonesian economists were initially development economists, more Keynesian than Friedmanian, although in recent years they have followed the international intellectual fashion to the right.) Instead, two considerations drove him again and again to accept their advice: first, the results in terms of economic growth that their policies produced; and second, his recognition that growth creates economic resources that he could use to build his political power base.[12]

Some of these resources were used to reward very large constituencies, such as rice farmers, who benefited for many years from irrigation rehabilitation programs and subsidies for seed, fertilizer, and pesticide, or urban consumers, who benefited from low or at least stable fuel and food prices. Road and bridge building, school and health center construction and staffing, and rural electrification provided millions of jobs and left behind improved infrastructure and services. Other resources have been targeted more narrowly, such as salary increases for civil servants or, at the very beginning of the New Order, distribution of free rice to soldiers. Still others have been used to buy the loyalty of high officials and military officers, either as outright gifts or as opportunities to make extra income, openly or covertly.

Finally, it is important to note that Suharto's alliance with Sino-Indonesian business was an important part of this story. Most large and even middle-sized businesses in Indonesia are owned and run by Sino-Indonesians. This has been a source of much resentment on the part of ordinary indigenous Indonesians, many of whom believe that they are charged high prices, denied jobs, and prevented from competing on equal terms. Sino-Indonesian individuals, however, have had for the most part very good relations with state officials, including the military. Long before the New Order, officials had begun to trade protection and favoritism (e.g., contracts for state business and trade licenses) for a share of business profits.

Suharto's own business relationship with Liem Sioe Liong, the New Order's most successful Sino-Indonesian businessman, began in the late 1950s, when Liem supplied various goods and services to the Semarang-based Diponegoro division of the army, then headed by Suharto. During the New Order, these relationships became a major source both of the personal wealth of many officers and officials and of the material resources with which friends and enemies could be rewarded and punished by Suharto and his lieutenants. This symbiotic relationship should have limited the willingness or ability of Suharto and other generals to use the Sino-Indonesians as scapegoats, although some scapegoating did in fact take place in the first half of 1998.

What Changed?

What accounts for the difference between the flexible, prepared-to-listen Suharto of earlier years and the anti-IMF Suharto of 1997–98? One frequently mentioned explanation is the president's need for a quick fix, for a policy change that would have raised the value of the rupiah against the U.S. dollar enough to enable private businesspeople to pay the installments due on their dollar-denominated loans and therefore to obtain the letters of credit needed to import the raw materials required for their manufacturing operations. "The people will rebel if there are high prices and no jobs," Suharto told a high official in February, explaining the attractiveness of the currency board idea.[13] In Suharto's view, neither the IMF's 50-point program nor any subsequent IMF proposal held out comparable hope for a rapid appreciation of the rupiah.

A second explanation has been that the 50-point IMF program gave Suharto too little wiggle room to juggle the various constituencies that have supported the New Order for the past three decades. It is true that the program called for a more far-reaching and thoroughgoing liberalization of the economy than any previous reform package. Perhaps Suharto agreed, without full consideration of the 50 points, with the belief that the very signing of the document would restore market confidence. As implementation began and the rupiah did not appreciate substantially, he had second thoughts. First he called for an IMF-Plus (i.e., a currency board), and then, more ominously, he argued that the IMF agreement was counter to Article 33 of the Indonesian Constitution. In Suharto's interpretation, Article 33 mandates a significant economic role for the state and cooperatives, in addition to private business.

My own explanation is more personal. I suspect that Suharto at age 76 (when the crisis began in July 1997) was no longer willing or able to distinguish between the interests of his family and his cronies and those of the nation. When the two diverged, as they did most dramatically since the beginning of the financial crisis in July 1997, Suharto chose to defend the interests of his family, of course under the ideological cover of the constitution and Indonesian cultural values. For most of the past 30 years, as I have argued above, Suharto tacked between the two poles of economic nationalism, as represented by Habibie's state entrepreneurialism and Ginandjar's private business protectionism, and the pro-market policies of the professional economists and foreign donors. Family demands were there for a long time, and they had been growing, but as recently as the late 1980s and early 1990s he was willing to sacrifice some family interests for the greater good, as defined for him by the economists. This time, perhaps in part because his wiggle room was indeed so narrow, he took his stand with his family and cronies.

Support for this proposition is necessarily circumstantial and subject to multiple interpretations. One important piece of evidence, in my view, appeared in a March 11 editorial in *Kompas,* the Indonesian national newspaper of record.[14] According to *Kompas,* in the negotiations over the 50-point program, the Indonesian side objected to IMF demands to (1) abolish the monopoly enjoyed since the beginning of the New Order by the state logistics agency Bulog over the marketing of several basic commodities (rice, the staple for most Indonesians, was excepted from this demand); (2) require that all banks be properly audited; (3) eliminate marketing cartels in cement, plywood, and paper; (4) withdraw protection for the so-called national car; and (5) dismantle trade regimes in the agricultural sector, particularly in clove marketing. Of these five items, four were clearly directed at significant interests of either Suharto's children (e.g., Tommy's national car and clove monopoly, Bambang's and Tutut's banks) or his cronies (e.g., Liem Sioe Liong's banks and cement monopoly, Bob Hasan's plywood monopoly). Only Bulog—where family and crony interests were also involved—could plausibly be argued to be a state institution that should be maintained for a larger national purpose, i.e., keeping down the prices of basic commodities purchased by most Indonesians.

The Future

There is, of course, no predicting the future, especially in as uncertain a situation as Indonesians now find themselves. As of this writing in June 1998, however, two quite divergent scenarios seem at least plausible: democratization and a return to military rule.

As recently as April 1998, democratization did not seem a plausible alternative. The armed forces appeared to be too strong and civil society, defined as the complex of social and political organizations outside the state, too weak. What has changed in the meantime is both our perception of the significant players and the choices made by them.

THE POLITICAL ROLE OF THE ARMY

During the New Order, the armed forces, particularly the army, were considered to be the heart of the political system, the effective "ruling party" behind the false front of the state party, Golkar, and the ostensibly democratic system of parliamentary elections. Active-duty army officers are members of a small, self-contained community, all of whose members are graduates of the Military Academy in Magelang, Central Java. They share a set of values about the virtues of military life (discipline, hierarchy, willingness to sacrifice for the common good) and a paternalistic conception of civil-military relations (the so-called dual-function doctrine) that accords them a special responsibility to save the Indonesian nation and state from its enemies, foreign and especially domestic. They believe that since the 1940s the many conspiracies and rebellions staged by regional separatists and extremists of the left (Communists), right (militant Islamists), and center (liberal democrats) have been defeated only because of unified, concerted military action. They are prepared to act again if necessary and justified much of their recent behavior—for example, against demonstrating university students—in these terms.

Army officers also share an interest in maintaining the political role that has brought them wealth and status in the larger society. In the

New Order, serving and retired senior officers have routinely been given positions in civilian government as cabinet ministers, governors, district heads, and diplomats. They have been active in politics, either through appointment to the armed forces delegations in Parliament and provincial and district legislatures, or through assignment to a leadership position in Golkar. To ensure their continued loyalty, business opportunities dependent on state largesse have been made available to retiring noncommissioned as well as commissioned officers.

The army probably has sufficient strength in numbers, organization, and capability to overcome its likely opponents, with a few exceptions like the East Timorese guerrillas. This is of course a relative matter, dependent on the strengths of those opponents, about which I will have something to say below. In absolute terms, however, the army is not large as a percentage of the total population (roughly 200,000 out of 200,000,000), and at least some of its troops are not well trained, officered, equipped, or provided with proper housing and other basic amenities. Since the current economic crisis began, there have been many unconfirmed reports of desertion and robbery by ordinary soldiers. The military police, it is widely believed, are busier than ever before.

Moreover, a shared ideology, common material and status interests, and sufficient organizational capacity do not imply that the army is internally united. On the day after Habibie's swearing-in as president, Lieutenant-General Prabowo Subianto, Suharto's son-in-law, was transferred from the powerful position of commander of the army's Strategic Reserve to a marginal post as commander of the Armed Forces Staff and Command School in Bandung, West Java. One Prabowo ally, Major-General Muchdi Purwopranyoto, was also immediately removed from his position as commander of Special Forces, while two others, the chief of staff of the Strategic Reserve and the Jakarta regional commander, were reassigned some weeks later. The apparent reason for the reassignments was an attempt by Prabowo to pressure President Habibie into promoting him to army chief of staff or even armed forces commander.

Since the late 1980s, the army has also been split into so-called green (the color of Islam) and red-and-white (the colors of the national flag, implying a suprareligious national unity) factions. General Benny Murdani, armed forces commander from 1983 to 1988 and a Roman Catholic, is alleged to have discriminated in his promotion and appointment policies against devoutly Islamic officers on the ground that they might favor turning Indonesia into an Islamic state. Murdani himself denies having had such a policy. By the mid-1990s, the issue had faded somewhat as Murdani had moved into the background, but Prabowo was sometimes identified as a leader of the greens and Wiranto, especially after he became army chief of staff in 1997, as a leader of the red-and-white faction. This division is likely to have continuing significance to the degree that civil society is polarized, as it is increasingly becoming, between two broad groups of Indonesians: Muslims who define their political interests in religious terms; and Muslims who do not, together with non-Muslim Indonesians (Christians, Hindu Balinese, and others).

The main source of army weakness today, however, is not military incompetence or internal splits but lack of political vision and leadership. In the past decade, President Suharto made all the key political decisions, allowing officers only an implementing role. In the early months of 1998 it became clear to close observers that no officer, including Wiranto and even the obviously politically ambitious Prabowo, had any independently formulated plan of action to deal with rising student and popular protest or Suharto's weakening grip on the political system. The result was a pattern of reaction instead of action. Since the transfer of power to Habibie, Wiranto and his chief of staff for social and political affairs, Lieutenant-General Bambang Susilo Yudhoyono, have begun to think in a more systematic way about the political future of the armed forces. Fortunately for the prospects for democratization, the two officers have stated that Indonesia should become a democracy and that the armed forces should no longer be a part of or provide campaign support to Golkar, a key element of the authoritarian New Order system. Wiranto has also begun to build a personal support base within the army and to forge an alliance with President Habibie.

CIVIL SOCIETY AND POLITICS

What of civil society outside the state? For three decades, organized opposition to the New Order was minuscule for several reasons. Indonesian society is pluralistic, even fragmented, with many antagonisms among groups that make it difficult for them to coalesce into organizations large enough to challenge the state. President Suharto repressed the demands of virtually all groups, but he also took advantage of their antagonisms by setting one group against another, much as he did with top army officers, to prevent the formation of powerful alliances. Equally important, economic development success made it possible for him to distribute material and status benefits widely, both to large groups like rice farmers and to individuals like the leaders of the nongovernment parties. As long as the benefits kept flowing, few desired to oppose the Father of Development, a title bestowed on Suharto by the Assembly in the 1970s.

In mid-1997, the benefits stopped flowing, and the opposition began to mobilize. While there was still little organization of the sort required in a democratic political system, there seemed to be widespread support—even an emerging consensus—for the idea of democracy. This was certainly true among the educated middle- and upper-class activists and the students, although the latter probably have only a shaky comprehension of democracy as concrete practice. We know less about the views of ordinary workers and farmers, although it is likely that because they have been kept apolitical for so long, their opinions are less well formed and they have little understanding of democracy. In the final analysis, what is perhaps most important is that from mid-1997 to mid-1998 the balance of political initiative shifted from the Suharto-dominated armed forces to political activists outside the state. The army without Suharto has been thrown off its guard, and civilians have moved into the vacuum created by the military's lack of vision and leadership.

Historically, Indonesians have tended to organize politically by religious, social class, and ethnic or regional affiliation. They did so openly from 1950 to 1959, under the democratic constitution of 1950. The influence of religion and social class was obvious in the 1955 parliamentary election, when the four major parties (which collectively received nearly 80 percent of the vote) represented middle- and upper-class groups associated with the state bureaucracy (the Nationalist Party [PNI]); urban and rural workers and landless farmers (the Communist Party [PKI]); modernist Muslims (Masyumi); and traditionalist Muslims (Nahdlatul Ulama, or NU, the Awakening of the Traditional Religious Teachers).

Modernist Muslims look directly to the Koran for their understanding of their religious obligations; sociologically they tend to be urban traders, professionals such as school teachers, or (increasingly today) civil servants. Traditionalist Muslims adhere to the classical Syafi'i school of Koranic interpretation; they tend to be small farmers or rural landlords. Of the four large parties, Masyumi best represented Indonesia's ethnic diversity, in part because there are large communities of modernists in Sumatra, Kalimantan, and Sulawesi as well as in West Java, the home of the ethnic Sundanese, and East and Central Java, the home of the ethnically dominant Javanese (who represent about half the total Indonesian population.) The other three large parties were all predominantly Java-based. There were also small Protestant and Catholic parties (Christians number about 9 percent of the population, Muslims

88 percent) and many ethnic-based parties able to win significant shares of the vote in their home regions.

These 1950s divisions are a useful (although hardly exact, given 40 years of social change) guide to political organization and mobilization in the 1990s. Most of the old Nationalist Party's state bureaucratic constituency has long since accepted the New Order; their children are today's civil servants and, at election time, have been Golkar cadres. There is significant antimilitary sentiment among this group but so far no willingness to act outside normal bureaucratic channels (where there has long been fierce civil-military competition for choice posts). Today's PDI is the linear descendant of the old Nationalist Party (it also incorporates the old Catholic and Protestant parties), but before Megawati Sukarnoputri's brief reign as party leader (1993–96), the PDI never attracted much attention. Megawati's own inability to articulate a political program different from the government is perhaps indicative both of her background and of the constituency she represents.

Working-class political aspirations have been harshly repressed throughout the New Order, which was born in the blood of hundreds of thousands of members and supporters of the Communist Party, who were killed by the military and by local anticommunists in 1965–66. Since the mid-1980s, the government's drive to develop export-oriented manufacturing industries has created a large new working class, centered around Jakarta and a few other large cities (Surabaya, Medan, and Semarang in particular). The new workers are disproportionately female, young, and newly arrived from neighboring rural areas. In the early 1990s, they began to protest low wages and poor working conditions, and the government has responded with a range of ameliorative (mainly raising wages), co-optative/coercive (organization by the state-controlled labor union), and repressive (arrests, torture, and killings of independent union organizers and wildcat strikers) measures. The current economic crisis could lead to a substantial increase in worker unrest and protest (although many of the now unemployed young female workers have returned to their villages), but it has not yet done so.

Among devout Indonesian Muslims, especially the generation under 40, the modernist-traditionalist cleavage appears to be declining in terms of actual patterns of religious beliefs and practices. Politically, however, the dichotomy continues to be represented by two huge associations and their respective leaders, both of whom are well known and popular in the larger society. The traditionalist association is NU, now a social and educational organization led by village and town-based Koranic teachers. (In the early 1950s, NU was part of Masyumi, from the mid-1950s to 1973 it was an independent political party, and from 1973 to 1984 it was part of the United Development Party.) NU's national leader is Abdurrahman Wahid (called Gus Dur), a religious pluralist and political democrat.

The modernist association is Muhammadiyah, an independent organization whose main activity is running private schools and hospitals. Its leader is Amien Rais, educated at Notre Dame and the University of Chicago, who also supports democratization but who has for most of his career displayed a narrower conception of religious truth and earned a reputation for hostility to Christians and other non-Muslims. Since the beginning of 1998, however, he has checked his anti-Christian, anti-Western rhetoric and reached out politically to non-Muslim Indonesians, including Sino-Indonesians, and to the non-Muslim international community on which Indonesia is now so dependent for economic assistance.

NU, founded in 1926, has a long history of accommodation to the ruler of the day, and has issued religious decrees (*fatwa*) accepting both Dutch colonial rule (in the 1930s) and President Sukarno's personal dictatorship (in the early 1960s). Gus Dur has combined this tradition with a search for ways to help create a modern democratic political system and society for Indonesia and simultaneously to bring NU members into that society. In the 1980s he worked closely with Armed Forces Commander Murdani. After Murdani's political decline in the late 1980s, Gus Dur became a more outspoken opponent of Suharto and an active promoter of democracy. For several years he played a leading role in the Forum Demokrasi, which attracted democratic activists of many different religious and ideological backgrounds. In 1997, under pressure both from the government and from the political conservatives who dominate NU at the local level, he reversed course. During the 1997 parliamentary election campaign, while ostensibly remaining nonpartisan, he took Golkar's Tutut on a tour of NU strongholds in East Java. In January 1998 Gus Dur suffered a stroke, and he did not participate in the political drama leading up to Suharto's resignation in May.

Muhammadiyah, founded in 1912, was affiliated with the Masyumi political party until Masyumi was banned in 1960, explicitly for involvement in the regional rebellions of the late 1950s but implicitly for promoting the idea of a state based on Islamic law. From 1960 until the early 1990s, Muhammadiyah stayed out of politics, partly from conviction that the organization's purposes were nonpolitical and partly because Islamic modernists were suspected by the government of continuing to harbor a desire for an Islamic state. In the early 1980s, Muhammadiyah and most other Muslim organization leaders signed an oath of loyalty to the state doctrine Pancasila, which mandates religious tolerance, and the cloud of suspicion began to lift. The organization remained nonpolitical, however, until Gadjah Mada University lecturer Amien Rais and a cohort of young, many Western-educated, intellectuals took the helm in 1994.

Amien's first national-level political move, even before he took over Muhammadiyah, was to join with many other modernists in the founding in 1990 of Ikatan Cendekiawan Muslim se-Indonesia (ICMI), the Indonesian Association of Muslim Intellectuals, an organization conceived by young modernist activists but immediately co-opted by Suharto. Because ICMI was headed (at Suharto's direction) by then Minister of Research and Technology Habibie, modernist activists believed that after many years in the political wilderness they would finally be able to play an influential role in government. For the most part these hopes were not realized while Suharto was president, although a few activists have been given positions in the new Habibie government.

Amien himself, however, was removed by Suharto from his post as chair of ICMI's Board of Experts in 1997. In the New Order, to play inside the system meant to refrain from serious public criticism, and Amien repeatedly criticized many aspects of the government's development program and other policies, including the absence of democracy. He questioned the first family's business ventures and repeatedly raised the issue of presidential succession. In early 1998, before the Consultative Assembly session, Amien called for Suharto to stand down and offered himself as a presidential candidate. After Suharto was elected president for his seventh term, Amien announced that Suharto had six months to a year to prove himself worthy of reelection. If the president failed to lead Indonesia out of the economic crisis by that time, Amien promised to lead a "people power" movement. Earlier in the year, Amien also proposed a grand opposition coalition to be led by himself, Megawati, and Gus Dur. Megawati signed on, but Gus Dur refused on the ground that this was not the time to anger the president or the army. Gus Dur's resistance was also rooted in a deeper historical hostility to modernists and to the Masyumi tradition, and perhaps also in personal dislike for Amien.

One other modernist Islamic group should be mentioned briefly, the militants associated with Dewan Dakwah Islamiyah Indonesia, the Indonesian Islamic Preaching Council, and with the Indonesian Committee for Solidarity with the Islamic World (KISDI). The Dewan Dakwah was founded by ex-Masyumi politicians who chose in the restricted political climate of the late 1960s to concentrate on religious activities. They publish an in-house magazine, *Media Dakwah* (*Preaching*

Medium), that is distributed to mosques and widely available in Islamic bookstores. KISDI is a newer, more overtly political organization, and spends much of its time demonstrating against domestic opponents or Western governments. The combined forces of Dewan Dakwah and KISDI are still small, but they are much more influential today than they were a decade ago.

The militants' objectives appear to be an Indonesian society more in conformity with a narrow construction of Islamic law; they also advocate a fiercely anti-Israeli, anti-American foreign policy.[15] Historically, few Indonesian Muslims have shared these objectives. For most of the New Order, the militants were the true "extreme right," suppressed by the government and hostile to it. Since the mid-1980s, however, and especially in the last few years, they have become more royalist than the king, defending Suharto, his ministers, and his policies against all comers. They appear to have been persuaded by a series of Suharto policies and gestures perceived as friendly to Islam, and by the president's own late-in-life pilgrimage to Mecca. They favored the appointment of Habibie as vice president but did not join the student agitation (which they claimed was Christian-influenced) against Suharto. After Habibie became president, they led the effort to dislodge the students occupying the Assembly building who were now calling for Habibie's resignation. They also picketed the American embassy, claiming that the United States had intervened in Indonesian politics by supporting the anti-Suharto movement.

What of regionally based ethnic groups, several of which rebelled against central control from the 1940s to the early 1960s? Perhaps two points should be made. First, most members of regional groups outside Java, for historical reasons having to do with the prewar nationalist movement and the 1945–49 revolution against the Dutch, have a strong sense of Indonesian identity. This is particularly true of the most populous regions, like the multiethnic provinces of North Sumatra and South Sulawesi. The widespread use of the national language, Bahasa Indonesia, has helped to strengthen this identity.

There are two provinces, however, where loyalty to Indonesia is limited or nonexistent: Irian Jaya, which was forcibly incorporated in 1962; and East Timor, seized in 1975. Both provinces have small populations and are remote from Jakarta and Java, so their importance should not be overestimated. Moreover, the armed opposition to Indonesia in Irian Jaya is small, poorly organized and equipped, and until now able to offer only sporadic resistance, especially given the weight of armed forces power in the region. East Timor is another matter. There, both clandestine organization and armed guerrilla activity appear to be on the rise. Moreover, the Indonesian government has been on the defensive internationally, especially since the 1991 massacre in East Timor's capitol, Dili, that left as many as 200 unarmed Timorese dead. One of Habibie's first moves as president was to try to defuse the Timor problem by offering autonomy to the province in return for acceptance by pro-independence Timorese of integration with Indonesia. Predictably, his offer was rejected, as the Timorese believe that they will be able to wring greater concessions, perhaps even agreement to an independence referendum, out of the Habibie government.

Second, a strong sense of national identity does not imply acceptance of centralized government policymaking. Since the late 1950s, when the steel frame of military control was constructed in many regions, most Outer Island residents have wanted greater autonomy from the center. Jakarta-based officers and officials (and not just Javanese ones), on the other hand, have tended to see separatists under every bed and have been reluctant to devolve even a small amount of power and authority. Thirty years of New Order development programs have made matters worse. They have undoubtedly brought greater prosperity to many, perhaps most, inhabitants. But they have also sharpened local ethnic, religious, and class cleavages, and created new antagonisms toward outsiders, without providing effective institutions through which aggrieved groups can press their claims. The numerous and widespread local eruptions of protest since 1995 are perhaps only precursors of greater explosions to come.

Finally, mention must be made of two groups that do not fit easily into my 1950s/1990s framework, but are or are becoming significant political actors: the indigenous entrepreneurial and managerial upper and middle classes, and university students. Both groups are much larger, absolutely and as a proportion of the population, today than they were in the 1950s. Both are also markedly more Islamic, as society as a whole has become more Islamic.

Throughout the New Order the entrepreneurs and managers have taken a backseat to officers and officials, who have controlled the (relatively) vast resources of the state. The reduced importance of oil to the Indonesian economy, plus accelerated trade and financial liberalization since the late 1980s, has given the private sector a bigger economic role. As a result, indigenous businesspeople have begun to demand more political representation as well. The election a few years ago of businessman Aburizal Bakrie as head of Kadin, the Chamber of Commerce and Industry, over a state enterprise official preferred by Suharto, was a straw in the wind. So was the appointment of Tanri Abeng, a highly respected private sector manager, to Suharto's last and Habibie's first cabinet as minister for the empowerment (that is, privatization) of state enterprises. The process is a gradual one, however, and is not likely to result any time soon in the takeover of the state by private businesspeople. Although most of the businesspeople are devout Muslims, their politics appear to have no specifically Islamic content.

University and even high school students played a critical role at the beginning of the New Order, providing much of the mobilized popular support that the army under then Major-General Suharto needed in its struggle to topple President Sukarno. Beginning in February 1998, as the campaign against Suharto's reelection escalated, students again began to mobilize on virtually every major state university campus and at many private universities as well. In Jakarta and Yogyakarta, tens of thousands of students—numbers scarcely imaginable even a few weeks earlier—listened approvingly to fiery antigovernment and anti-Suharto speeches. At Gadjah Mada University, Suharto was burned in effigy. Most of these students appear to come from devout Muslim families, and many are from outside Java. Their largest organization, created in the heat of the anti-Suharto struggle, is the Action Front of Indonesian Muslim Students (KAMMI), whose name consciously echoes the largest anti-Sukarno organization of the mid-1960s, Action Front of Indonesian Students (KAMI). KAMMI's first cadres came from the well-connected network of student mosques that exist on all university campuses. Despite its origins and name, however, none of KAMMI's demands was specifically Islamic but instead reflected the anti-Suharto, pro-IMF, prodemocracy sentiments of the protest movement as a whole.

HABIBIE'S POLICIES

President Habibie's first political moves have on balance contributed to the strengthening of civilians and the weakening of the military as a political force, and have improved the prospects for democratization. Habibie is of course himself a civilian and has put mostly civilians into government positions. More important, however, has been his commitment to both economic and political reform, as those concepts are understood in Indonesia today.

Economic reform means full acceptance of the policies recommended by the IMF and other foreign lenders, which it is hoped will lead to a strengthening of the banking system, resolution of the private debt problem, and finally an appreciation of the rupiah sufficient to restart economic growth. Although this policy has yet to show tangible results, it is widely understood in Indonesia that there is no other course. Habibie has convincingly demonstrated his commitment by keeping on an old political enemy, Coordinating Minister for the Economy Ginandjar, one of the few officials who has the trust of the IMF, and by bringing back into his government the professional economists, including Professor Wijoyo, whose policies were responsible for three decades of sustained economic growth during the New Order.[16] He has also reached out to Sino-Indonesians, whose participation in the reconstruction of the economy is essential, by assuring them that "we are all Indonesians and live on Indonesian soil; we do not recognize differences of ethnicity, religion and race."[17]

On the political front, Habibie has responded to demands for democratization by promising to implement a four-step process: (1) passage by Parliament, sometime in early 1999, of new laws to enable free and fair elections and open party competition; (2) calling a special session of the Consultative Assembly at the end of 1998 to set a new date for elections; (3) holding parliamentary elections in the middle of 1999; and (4) calling a regular session of the Consultative Assembly at the end of 1999 to elect a new president and vice president and set the "broad outlines of state policy," as mandated by the 1945 constitution, for the next five years. He has also announced that the restrictive press law will be withdrawn and that in the meantime all Indonesians are free to establish new media.

With these promises and some early actions (for example, the release of several New Order political prisoners and the drafting of democratic election law proposals by the Departments of Justice and Home Affairs), Habibie has managed to win considerable, if tentative, legitimation for his incumbency as a transitional president. National political debate has shifted away from such issues as whether the transfer of power from Suharto to Habibie was constitutional and whether Habibie's presidency is or is not simply a continuation of Suharto's New Order. The focus now is on types of electoral and party systems. Should a democratic Indonesia continue with the proportional representation electoral system in use throughout the New Order, or should it move to some form of majoritarian system? Should political parties based on ethnicity or religion be allowed, or should all parties in principle be open to all Indonesians?

Habibie's political reform program has received crucial support from the military under Wiranto and his chief of staff for social and political affairs, Lieutenant-General Susilo Bambang Yudhoyono. Indeed, a kind of de facto alliance has been formed, in which Habibie's dependence on armed forces support for his reform program, so far provided by Wiranto, is matched by Wiranto's dependence on Habibie, his constitutional commander-in-chief, for his continuation as armed forces commander. Wiranto appears to recognize that he has cast his personal lot with Habibie and that if the latter were to be replaced, say by a special session of the Assembly convened by Habibie's enemies in Golkar, then he would in turn be replaced by the new president. As a transitional figure, Habibie also has the de facto support of the arguably (none has yet been tested in a free election) most popular civilian politicians, Amien Rais of Muhammadiyah, Abdurrahman Wahid of NU, and Megawati Sukarnoputri of PDI. These three leaders appear to have given up scheming to overthrow Habibie in the short run and instead are concentrating their energies on building parties and a coalition that can win majority support in the postelection Assembly.

This is not to argue that the road to elections or to a democratic Indonesia will be smooth. Akbar Tanjung, minister in charge of the State Secretariat (that is, Habibie's chief of staff) and Habibie's choice to lead Golkar through the reform process, reportedly has said that national politics is now a jungle full of dangerous animals. Habibie's personal support remains weak, and his coalition is fragile. If he makes a tactical mistake, his strategy could fail, and he himself could be overthrown before elections are held. If he does succeed, the prospects for democratic consolidation will depend heavily on the nature of the party system and the political leadership that emerges from the elections. For example, in a worst-case scenario, worse even than the multiparty system of the 1950s, the new Parliament might consist of many small parties whose leaders have no national vision or sense of common purpose and whose squabbling quickly persuades the armed forces leaders that once again only they can save the state and nation. Conversely, major leaders outside the government could begin to build the kinds of links among themselves and their organizations that will translate at the end of 1999 into a stable governing coalition.

Conclusion

There is, particularly at the elite level, a strong Hobbesian streak in modern Indonesian political culture: the belief that most Indonesians cannot be entrusted with extensive personal liberties or with the right to participate in political life on their own terms but must instead be persuaded or forced in their own interest to accept the superior wisdom of a paternalistic elite. In the late 1960s, as the New Order began to take shape, Suharto took advantage of this belief, offering prosperity and stability in exchange for acceptance of authoritarian government.

Most, although of course not all, Indonesians appeared at the time willing to accept the offer. In return, they received 30 years of steady economic growth, an achievement beyond most people's wildest expectations. During this period, they were frequently reminded of the government's willingness to use force against its opponents, including not only extremists of the right and left but also advocates of a more democratic Indonesia. They have also been reminded that the particular growth path they have followed has had many social and environmental costs and—with great force since mid-1997—that it has made them vulnerable to sometimes capricious international economic and political winds.

Today Indonesians are paying the price for their Hobbesian bargain with Suharto: an economic decline steeper than that of any of their East Asian neighbors and great difficulty in managing the leadership succession. The contrast is particularly obvious with Thailand and South Korea, both of which quickly changed their political leaders and got back on track economically. It is probably not accidental that in both countries a decades-long popular struggle produced, well in advance of the current crisis, democratic political processes and institutions that made it possible to choose a new prime minister or president who could count on broad popular support for his policies. Indonesia now has—almost miraculously, given the strength of the military and the weakness of civil society under Suharto—a genuine opportunity to create its own democratic processes and institutions. But we should not underestimate the obstacles in the road ahead or the real probability of a return to armed forces rule, including perhaps another Hobbesian bargain, in the relatively near future.

Notes

1. Confidential interview, Jakarta, March 9, 1998.
2. Goenawan Mohamad, *Catatan Pinggir*, vol. III (Jakarta: Grafiti, 1991), p. 121.
3. See Human Rights Watch, *Indonesia Alert: Economic Crisis Leads to Scapegoating of Ethnic Chinese* (New York: Human Rights Watch, February 1998).
4. *Kompas*, March 21, 1998, p. 1.
5. See R. William Liddle, "The Year of Deja Vu," *Asian Wall Street Journal*, October 3, 1997.
6. Confidential interviews, Jakarta, February 5–6, 1998.
7. *Forum Keadilan*, June 15, 1998, p. 23.
8. Salim Said, "Suharto's Armed Forces: Building a Power Base in New Order Indonesia 1966–1998," *Asian Survey*, June 1998.

9. *Kompas*, May 22, 1998, p. 5.
10. For an excellent account of each of these events, see John Bresnan, *Managing Indonesia* (New York: Columbia University Press, 1993).
11. Suharto, *Pikiran, Ucapan dan Tindakan Saya: Otobiografi* (Jakarta: Citra Lamtoro Gung Persada, 1988).
12. For a fuller exposition of this argument, see R. William Liddle, *Leadership and Culture in Indonesian Politics* (Sydney: Allen and Unwin, 1996), ch. 4.
13. Confidential interview, 12 March 1998. For a sympathetic treatment of Suharto's plight, see George Melloan, "What, Exactly, Does Clinton Want from Indonesia?" *Wall Street Journal*, March 10, 1998, p. A23.
14. "Paket Reformasi Ekonomi IMF Menjurus kepada Ekonomi Liberal," *Kompas*, March 11, 1998, p. 4.
15. The KISDI point of view may be accessed on the World Wide Web at http://www.kisdi.com.
16. Ginandjar's turnaround, from protectionist to free-marketeer, since the financial crisis began last July, is testimony to his political agility.
17. *Kompas*, May 27, 1998, p. 1.

3

Islam and Nation in the Post-Suharto Era

ROBERT W. HEFNER

IT IS A TRUISM of Indonesian studies that since the 1980s Indonesia has experienced a historically unprecedented Islamic revival. When evidence of this development first came to the attention of Western specialists on Indonesia, many were skeptical, convinced that state and society were so thoroughly dominated by *abangan* (literally meaning "red," the word refers to nonpracticing or nominal Muslims of Javanese ethnicity) that no such cultural transformation was possible. A half generation on, however, most observers now agree that a significant change in the social standing of Islam occurred in the second half of the Suharto era. Where observers disagree is in evaluating the implications of the Islamic resurgence for Indonesia's future. Does the resurgence augur poorly for Indonesia's remarkable heritage of religious and ethnic pluralism? Or might it play a positive role in efforts to deepen social supports for democracy, tolerance, and human rights? How much will the answer to these questions depend upon Indonesia's rulers themselves?

These are dauntingly expansive questions, a proper assessment of which would require a more extensive discussion than possible in a short paper. In this chapter, however, I will attempt a preliminary answer to these questions by sifting through the debris of the now defunct New Order for clues as to the likely role of Islam in post-Suharto Indonesia. In particular, I will examine the forms taken by the Islamic resurgence, social influences on its ideals and practice, and the relationship of both to the broader political-economic forces transforming Indonesia today.

To anticipate my conclusion, let me say that the answer to these questions depends largely on the way in which Indonesia's rulers exploit the allegiances of the revitalized but divided Muslim community. Contrary to some portrayals,[1] there is no single, civilization-wide pattern of Muslim politics, but a variety of competing organizations and ideals. The modern era's nation making and market globalization have, if anything, only increased the pluralism and contestation of politics in the Muslim world. As a result, the most significant "clash of cultures" today is not that between distinct civilizations but, as in Algeria, Iran, and many other nations, between rival political traditions within the same country. It is just such a contest between different visions of Islam that hangs in the balance in today's Indonesia. Despite the bitter legacy of the Suharto regime and despite deep divides among Indonesian Muslims, however, the balance of forces in this country still favors the development of a civil and democratic Islam.

The Forms and Meanings of Resurgence

In their masterful *Muslim Politics,* Dale Eickelman and James Piscatori have observed that a central feature of Muslim politics throughout today's world is a struggle over "the interpretation of symbols and control of the institutions, formal and informal, that produce and sustain them."[2] A widely noted feature of this contest has been what the authors call the "objectification" of religious knowledge and, with it, the pluralization of religious authority. In contrast to an age when Islamic knowledge was the secure monopoly of a small number of erudite jurists (*ulama*), Islamic knowledge and practice today are objects of interest for growing numbers of ordinary people. In a manner that recalls Benedict Anderson's remarks on the influence of print capitalism on European nationalism,[3] Eickelman and Piscatori observe that this objectification of knowledge has been abetted by the expansion of mass higher education, the emergence of vast markets for inexpensive Islamic books and newspapers, and the displacement of orderly rural societies by unsettled urban ones.[4] Other, more general social changes have also contributed to this change in Muslim politics. Migration, education, and the growth of anonymous urban landscapes, for example, have weakened the established structures of popular society at the same time that religious scholars (*ulama*) have lost their monopoly on religious authority. The result is that throughout the Muslim world, populist preachers, neotraditionalist Sufi masters, and secularly educated "new Muslim intellectuals" vie with state-sponsored scholars to define just what Islam should be.[5] In some countries, the resulting "fragmentation of authority"[6] has pluralized social power and been a force for democratization.[7] Where the contest of carriers has coincided with civil war, economic collapse, ethnic polarization, or severe state violence, however, the struggle has sometimes abetted the ascent of a harsh "neofundamentalism" inimical to pluralism, women's emancipation, and a Muslim civil society.[8]

The resurgence in Indonesia resembles that of other Muslim countries but also has several distinctive features. One commonality is that the Suharto government's programs of mass education had a powerful influence on the Islamic resurgence. Between 1965 and the early 1990s, the percentage of young adults with basic literacy skills skyrocketed from about 40 percent to 90 percent.[9] The increase in the percentage of people completing senior high school was equally dramatic, rising from approximately 4 percent in 1970 to more than 30 percent today.[10]

By themselves, of course, higher levels of education do not predict heightened religiosity; indeed, as Robert Wuthnow and others have shown,[11] in the West higher education tended to coincide with the growth of secularism in political affairs. Several things were distinctive, however, about the relationship of mass education to the religious resurgence in Indonesia. First, the educational expansion occurred after 1966, when national regulations stipulating that all students undergo religious education were revised and vigorously enforced. The results of this strict policy were vividly apparent in the East Javanese villages where I worked in the 1970s and 1980s.[12] Before Suharto came to power in 1966, elementary schools in nominally Islamic villages had either ignored the regulations requiring religious education or implemented them in a casual manner. Some villages even hired *abangan* Javanists to teach the state's religious courses. But by the early 1970s, all elementary students were receiving the same mandatory religious instruction from state-certified teachers using state-published textbooks.

A few hours of religious instruction each week, of course, are not sufficient to effect a historically unprecedented Islamic resurgence. A second influence on the Indonesian resurgence, however, was that the expansion of Islamic institutions occurred at a time when many Indonesians were searching for a new moral framework to make sense of their rapidly changing society. Post-1966 changes in consumption, communications, education, and politics undermined locally based hierarchies and values.[13] Even in remote areas of the archipelago, villagers were introduced to nationally disseminated products, fashions, and political ideas. The heightened presence of the state and the muting or elimination of the party-based political structures of the 1950s also worked to weaken local structures of patronage and prestige and the secure cultural identities of which they were once part. The change led local elites to invest their resources, not in local relationships, but in consumer items, education, and capital goods capable of serving as currency in the national marketplace. In a few areas, such as Aceh, Irian Jaya, and East Timor, this development prompted defensive counterassertions of ethnic and regional identity. Elsewhere, however, the reaction has been more accommodating, and local lifestyles and traditions have become notably more Indonesian.

A third influence on the Indonesian resurgence is related to this heightening of state power and weakening of local tradition. As Adam Schwarz has observed,[14] for many Indonesians "Islam is seen as a safe alternative to the heavily circumscribed political structure." Throughout the New Order era, mosques, Islamic schools, and Muslim publications offered Indonesians some of the best opportunities for open discussions of public issues. Elsewhere the New Order state imposed strict limits on all forms of public participation. After political protests in January 1974, the regime cracked down on the national news media. In 1978 it imposed draconian restrictions on campus political activity. Between 1984 and 1985, the government required religious and other "mass" organizations (*organisasi massa*) to incorporate the Pancasila state ideology into their organizational charters; those that refused were banned. The Suharto regime also regularly interfered in the affairs of religious organizations, forcing them to ratify state policies and elect leaders acceptable to the regime. The regime's attempt in late 1994 to remove the liberal-minded reformer Abdurrahman Wahid from the leadership of Nahdlatul Ulama was one of the more brazen examples of this interference (see below).

Despite government meddling, Muslim organizations proved themselves capable of maintaining a greater measure of autonomy vis-à-vis the state than most public organizations. In their campaigns against the national sports lottery and government regulations on marriage,[15] and in support of Islamic banking and *halal* (religiously pure) food labeling, among others, Muslim organizations were able to exercise a decisive influence on government policies. By contrast, at least until its final months in 1997–98, the New Order regime demonstrated an unrelenting ability to control campus activism, labor organizations, and even business associations.[16] The regime also succeeded in reducing the two nominally independent political parties, the nationalist-oriented Indonesian Democratic Party (PDI) and the Muslim-oriented United Development Party (PPP), to ineffectual marginality. In this tightly controlled political landscape, then, Muslim social organizations were among the few capable of providing critical public engagement.

A fourth feature of the Islamic resurgence is related to state efforts to circumscribe the forms of religious expression. Although the Islamic resurgence in Indonesia shares the fragmentation of religious authority seen in many other Muslim countries, the religious scene also shows certain standardized or integrating characteristics. The most important of these bear the clear imprint of state policy. With its regulations recognizing only five faiths (Islam, Protestantism, Catholicism, Hinduism, and Buddhism) as legitimate options for its citizens, the New Order state effectively outlawed indigenous religions, once practiced in local communities across eastern Indonesia, Kalimantan, and interior Sumatra. Anthropologists working in these areas in the 1970s and 1980s provided vivid accounts of the deleterious impact of these policies on indigenous religions and, conversely, their role as a catalyst for conversion to Christianity or Islam.[17]

State policies have had an equally powerful effect on the less-orthodox profession of Islam. As Paul Stange's studies of the Sumarah movement in Javanese mysticism have shown, in the 1980s even mystical organizations (*aliran kepercayaan, kebatinan*) favored by some of the Javanese elite (including at one time the president) found themselves on the defensive in the face of state policies and an ascendant Islam. Although some openly presented themselves as alternatives to Islam in the 1950s,[18] by the late 1980s most mystical organizations felt obliged to present themselves as supporters, rather than opponents, of normative Islam.[19]

Ethnographic studies from rural Java paint a similar picture of the impact of the resurgence on folk Islam. Over the past 30 years, the institutions that once allowed Javanism to operate as a public alternative to orthodox Islam have declined, while institutions of Islamic worship and education have expanded. Thus, for example, the lavish communal rituals (*slametan desa*) once celebrated by Javanists at village spirit shrines (*dhanyang*) have disappeared from most communities, although in some areas private, individual celebrations survive.[20] Upset by Muslim organizations' participation in the anticommunist massacres of 1965–66,[21] some Javanists—perhaps 5 percent of the ethnic Javanese population as a whole—converted to Hinduism or Christianity in the first years of the New Order.[22] Others took refuge under the organizational canopy of mystical associations. Both developments pale, however, by comparison with the growing numbers of Javanists who have adopted a more conventional profession of Islam.

Indonesian observers have long suspected that this change in the situation of mystical organizations and nominal Muslims may well have serious political implications. In the 1950s, for example, nominal Muslims made up the core constituency of the Indonesian Communist Party and the left wing of the Indonesian Nationalist Party; opposition to orthodox Islam was one of the rallying cries of the populist left. Hence the conversion of large numbers of nominal Muslims to a more orthodox Islam could well represent a significant change in the political landscape.

But the consequences of the Islamic resurgence are more complex than a simple shift from secular nationalism to "conservative" Islam. Although precise statistical information is lacking, ethnographic evidence suggests that at an individual level many Indonesians, including many pious Muslims, remain relatively indifferent to state-sanctioned forms of religion. As the growing interest in Sufi mysticism among the middle class has illustrated, many prefer a do-it-yourself Islamo-spirituality to the developmental Islam of the state. It is important to emphasize that this popular interest in mysticism has less to do with the putative hold of ancient "Hindu-Buddhist" ideals on Indonesian culture—the influence of which was greatly exaggerated in postwar studies of Indonesian society—than with the pervasive concern of many ordinary Indonesians with personal autonomy and ethical self-determination.

Equally important, as the involvement of Muslim students in the overthrow of President Suharto in May 1998 illustrated, many pious youth have looked to Islam as a source of democratic and egalitarian values. Indeed, although a few conservative Islamists reject constitutional government, the ideals of national citizenship, and the concept of universal human rights, the more remarkable feature of the Indonesian political landscape is that since the early 1980s Muslim activists have been the primary public carriers of democratic ideals.[23] Pro-democracy Muslims were the single largest constituency involved in the effort to overthrow Suharto. Their leaders—Amien Rais, Nurcholish Madjid, Abdurrahman Wahid, and the many brave students who remained anonymous so as to avoid being kidnapped or killed—demonstrated a practical understanding of democracy and peaceful resistance that was nothing less than exemplary. For these and other reasons, it is important not to assume that the Islamic resurgence is ideologically uniform or, least of all, antithetical to democratization.

Traditionalists and Modernists

The final point to emphasize regarding the forms and meanings of Indonesia's Islamic resurgence concerns its class profile. Speaking of the situation in the Middle East, the French scholar Olivier Roy has argued that the politically mobilized wing of the Islamist resurgence has typically been based on an alliance of, on one hand, the socially disenfranchised urban poor and, on the other, downwardly mobile Muslim intellectuals, most of whom received technical training in state schools only to enter the ranks of the unemployed.[24] Applied to Indonesia, this characterization is much too simple, but it raises several issues worth considering.

During the first years of the New Order, the already fragmented Islamic leadership split further along ideological and generational lines. The most stable of the major Muslim groupings remained the traditionalist Nahdlatul Ulama (NU).[25] Despite internal disputes and repeated government attempts to weaken the organization, the NU leadership maintained its mass base. Building on an organization first developed in the 1950s, NU has a distinctive bifurcated leadership. The arrangement links well-educated and ideologically savvy urban activists to a poorer, nonactivist, and moderately conservative rural leadership, most of whom direct Koranic boarding schools (*pesantren*). From the outside, this peculiar alliance strikes many observers as implausibly unstable. Under the direction of a series of skilled NU leaders, however, the arrangement has proved itself capable of weathering the fiercest political storms.

Part of the key to NU's staying power has to do with the culture of its followers. Having evolved in a Javanese social environment, most of the membership is deeply imbued with populist or progressive nationalist sentiments, a point well documented in Andrée Feillard's and Martin van Bruinessen's recent studies of the organization.[26] Equally important, the rural Javanese who make up NU's base are relatively tolerant of variations in the profession of Islam—as long as the variations do not involve attacks on the sanctity of Islam itself (a line over which the Communist Party in the 1950s regularly trod).

During the 1980s and 1990s, NU's brilliant and charismatic leader, Abdurrahman Wahid, sought to bring the two wings of the organization into greater collaboration. He hoped to use the intellectual and organizational skills of the urban activists to transform the poor but tolerant mass base. Not surprisingly, the results of this ambitious effort have been mixed. On one hand, Wahid has succeeded in turning the national headquarters of his organization into a center for pro-democracy criticism of the government and the Muslim community itself. Equally important, in contrast to Suharto's attempts at manipulating the sentiments of conservative Muslims against the Chinese (see below), Wahid has been unfailing in his efforts to reassure religious and ethnic minorities that they are valued members of Indonesian society.

On the other hand, however, Wahid has had notably less success in improving the economic circumstances of NU's membership. Despite several well-intended initiatives,[27] NU's base remains the poorest and least educated segment of the Muslim community. In spite of Wahid's efforts, therefore, the culture of NU's urban wing has been only partially integrated into the rural mass organization. In the 1990s, the resulting fault line in NU did not escape the attention of Suharto strategists. Several times they sought to exploit it so as to block Wahid's pro-democracy efforts (see below).

Indonesia's modernist Muslims have a more uniform social profile than the traditionalists. The modernists are more urban, more affluent, and better educated. Despite their relative cultural homogeneity, however, the modernists have long been plagued by ideological divisions every bit as severe as the traditionalists'. Most famously, since the 1970s the senior leadership that led the modernist Muslim party Masyumi starting in the 1950s has been pitted against a smaller but socially ascendant group of new Islamic intellectuals.[28] The latter distanced themselves from the party organizations directed by senior modernist leaders. Indeed, some of the younger intellectuals have opposed the establishment of Islamic parties, calling instead for a "cultural" strategy of Islamic revitalization, focusing on the deepening of Muslim values in society rather than conquest of the state.[29]

This dispute between junior and senior modernists was influenced by differences of class and social status as well as generation and ideology. In the early 1950s, senior figures like Muhammad Natsir, Moehammad Roem, and Anwar Harjono had invested heavily in constitutional politics and the electoral road to power. As Allan Samson's research in the late 1960s showed,[30] when these leaders saw their prospects for electoral triumph fade in the late 1950s, their authority was challenged by theological conservatives in Masyumi, the party with which most Indonesian modernists were affiliated. During these same years, the business community that had earlier financed Masyumi's activities went into decline as inflation and the infrastructural collapse savaged the national economy. Although many in the old Muslim middle class hoped to see their fortunes revive under the New Order, the ruling elite struck most of its deals, not with Muslim entrepreneurs, but with Sino-Indonesians and, later, the children of the ruling elite themselves.[31]

Once the champions of a bright Islamic social democracy, in the late 1960s the senior modernist leadership responded to this crisis in their constituency by moving down market, directing their appeals at the urban poor and lower–middle class rather than the Muslim middle class. This shift in audience was especially apparent in the pronouncements of the organization most directly heir to the Masyumi mantle, the Dewan Dakwah Islamiyah Indonesia (Indonesian Council for Islamic Predication), or DDII. Hardened by political persecution and marginalized from economic life, the DDII directed its appeals toward a poorer and less-educated social base. It promoted Islamic law and ritual piety as a panacea for society's ills. In harsh and uncompromising terms, it also denounced conspicuous consumption, governmental corruption, Javanese mysticism, Muslim liberalism, and the economic dominance of the Chinese. In its most florid pronouncements, the DDII identified all of these things as agents of a vast conspiracy to "Christianize" Indonesia.[32]

In the last five years of his rule, Suharto courted conservative Muslims and attempted to suppress the activities of pro-democracy Muslims. Responding to the president's overtures, the DDII and its affiliates slowly reconciled with the regime. The DDII's transformation from a principled if conservative Islamist critic to regime supporter was essentially complete by 1996.[33] The change was in part the result of a secret lobbying campaign of DDII leaders by representatives of the Center for Policy and Development Studies (CPDS), a think tank linked at the time to the "Muslim generals" Prabowo, Hartono, and Feisal Tanjung. CPDS lobbyists mounted their campaign by first winning the support of Ahmad Sumargono—the fiery leader of the Indonesian Committee for Solidarity with the Islamic World, known by its acronym KISDI (an organization with fraternal ties to the DDII leadership). Sumargono then acted as a lobbyist to the DDII leadership.

From this point on, the DDII continued to criticize the government on a few issues, most notably what DDII officials regarded as the government's tendency to give unfair economic advantages to ethnic Chinese. In public statements, however, the DDII leadership took pains not to criticize President Suharto himself; indeed they regularly praised him for supporting Muslim religious interests. The message seemed to be that Catholics, secularists, Javanists, and the Chinese were responsible for the New Order's abuses, not Suharto.

The younger Islamic intellectuals who rose to prominence in the 1970s and 1980s had a very different social profile. Although many had been born into the old Muslim middle class, most directed their appeals toward the new Muslim middle class, concentrated, not in trade and independent enterprise, but in education, the state bureaucracy, and state-sponsored businesses. The educated and urban profile of these new Muslim leaders made them open to new currents in Islamic thought, including activist-oriented Islamic writing from South Asia and the Middle East, and Western scholarship on democracy and modernity. From a comparative Islamic perspective, the depth and breadth of Muslims' engagement with the latter literature is remarkable. Since the late 1980s, the largest audience for democratic and pluralist ideas in Indonesia has been, not secular nationalists, but reform-minded Muslim democrats.[34] Nowhere in the Muslim world have Muslim intellectuals engaged the ideas of democracy, civil society, pluralism, and the rule of law with a vigor and confidence equal to that of Indonesian Muslims.

Lacking an independent economic base, however, and appealing to a constituency with strong ties to the bureaucracy, these new Islamic intellectuals were also vulnerable to pressures from the Suharto regime. Nowhere was this vulnerability clearer than in the organization created by Suharto in December 1990 to serve as the vehicle of the new Islamic intellectuals, the Indonesian Association of Muslim Intellectuals (ICMI). ICMI represented a brazen attempt on the part of the Suharto regime to co-opt and control Indonesian Islam. It would also prove to be one of the regime's most astounding failures.

From Revitalization to Co-optation

ICMI's creation was the result of a complex convergence of social forces.[35] Among them were the Islamic revival; the growth of an educated and prosperous middle class; and, in the late 1980s, President Suharto's interest in courting a base of support beyond the armed forces. Together these developments pushed Islam to the center of Indonesian politics, a center from which it had been barred for 25 years.

We know that the president made his rapprochement with Muslims in part so as to counterbalance his worsening relationship with high-ranking officers in the armed forces, especially the influential (and Catholic) former minister of defense and commander of the armed forces Benny Murdani. Once the most powerful man in the Indonesian military, in the late 1980s Murdani dared to question the president about his family's corrupt business activities. As with previous challengers, Suharto did not take kindly to the criticism. He launched a merciless campaign to neutralize the general's influence in the armed forces and sought to counterbalance military power with that of the Muslim community.

Some American political scientists have spoken as if the president's anxiety about Murdani were the only influence on his gestures toward Muslims. What this analysis overlooks is that the overtures continued long after Murdani was forced out of office. Although it correctly highlights tensions with the military, the analysis is also too narrow in that it fails to explain just why the president came to see Muslims as a significant force in the first place. From my own interviews with several of his ministers, however, it is clear that by the mid-1980s the president was already aware of and concerned about the growing Islamic resurgence. On several occasions during those years he is said to have expressed a desire to avoid a confrontation with Islam like that occurring in other Muslim countries. In the 1980s, he and his advisers reflected regularly on events in Iran; in the early 1990s, they discussed the crisis in Algeria. The president is said to have taken these examples to heart, and ICMI was the result.

ICMI was bitterly opposed by many in the military and, most interestingly, the Nahdlatul Ulama. Supporters of democratic reform in the latter organization regarded ICMI not as a vehicle for Muslim penetration of the state but for state penetration of Islam; they feared it would kidnap the Muslim social movement just as the latter was beginning to exercise social influence. Abdurrahman Wahid, the NU leader, had worked for 10 years to transform his organization into a vehicle of grass-roots development and pluralist moderation. Having dedicated himself to this effort, Wahid was disappointed to see the government courting Muslim leaders he regarded as ultraconservative.[36] Wahid repeatedly warned that the president was playing with fundamentalist fire, remarks that were said to have infuriated the president.

Other leaders of the Muslim community, however, especially in the ranks of theological modernists, welcomed ICMI's establishment, although not without ambivalence. In private, many expressed concern about the president's motives, fearing he might succeed in coopting regime critics. Having been marginalized from national politics for a quarter century, however, it is not surprising that others among the modernist leadership found the prospect for even limited influence tempting. Anwar Haryono, a high-ranking member of Masyumi and the DDII who in the 1980s had been active in the dissident "Petition of 50" group, put aside his reservations to collaborate with the government, hopeful that the president's gestures were a harbinger of better things to come. He and his followers justified their actions by citing a series of concessions to Muslims made by the president between 1988 and 1993. These included the founding of an Islamic bank, expansion of the authority of Islamic courts, the lifting of the prohibition on the Islamic veil (*jilbab*) in schools, the founding of an Islamic newspaper, the abolition of the state-run sports lottery, greater Muslim programming on television (including lessons in the Arabic language), increased funding for Muslim schools and mosques, and the replacement of the

Catholic general Benny Murdani as head of the armed forces with generals regarded as more sympathetic to Islam.[37] Among conservative and moderate Muslims, there was talk of a "honeymoon" with the president.

In political terms, however, the opening to the Muslim community was always highly circumscribed. From the beginning, Muslims regarded as critical of the regime were excluded from the ranks of those granted presidential favor. Even those who agreed to cooperate with the regime found themselves subject to continuing controls. During the months leading up to ICMI's founding, for example, observers expected the chairmanship of the organization to be given to Dawam Rahardjo. Rahardjo is an intelligent, independent, and eminently moderate Muslim who had worked for years in nongovernmental circles. To supporters of ICMI outside government, Rahardjo embodied the virtues of intellectual sophistication and political moderation to which they expected ICMI to be dedicated. To the disappointment of Muslim independents, however, the chairmanship was awarded not to Rahardjo but to Minister of Research and Technology B. J. Habibie, one of the president's closest advisers. Although Habibie was known to be moderately pious, he had never been a leader in the Muslim community or otherwise displayed an interest in Islamic public affairs. He was best known, not for his Islamic credentials, but for his commitment to expensive programs of state-subsidized industrialization. By the late 1980s, his ventures in airplane construction, shipbuilding, and other "strategic industries" were estimated to drain hundreds of millions of dollars from the annual budget. By the late 1980s, no one in the inner circle enjoyed the president's favor as much as Habibie. And no one had a reputation for being more loyal.

For Suharto, Habibie's merit lay in his subservient loyalty and in the fact that Muslim leaders perceived him as sympathetic to their concerns. The other figure whose name was broached as a possible ICMI chairman was Emil Salim, a former minister. Salim was a skilled economist, a pious (and liberal) Muslim, and a person of sterling character. He was also known, however, to have serious misgivings about the first family's economic dealings and the president himself. (As Indonesia's political crisis deepened in 1997–98, Salim moved quickly into opposition and proved one of the president's boldest critics.) Habibie had none of these reservations. He also had no independent power base, making him all the more dependent on presidential favor. Moreover, with his dreamy plans for catapulting Indonesia into a high-tech future, Habibie appealed to the side of Suharto that saw government patronage as an important ingredient in economic progress.

Independent Muslims in ICMI were aware that Habibie's charge was to win their support while ensuring that rank-and-file members did not overstep the bounds of allowable dissent. However, in the early 1990s, they and other Indonesians hoped that the president might finally be relaxing his grip on politics. They also hoped that Habibie's vivacious personal energy might prove infectious and encourage the greying Suharto to loosen up. The decision to marginalize Rahardjo and other independents from positions of power in ICMI, however, was an early sign that Habibie's vivaciousness was not in fact an indicator of genuine openness. An ill omen in this regard occurred in 1992 with the founding of the ICMI newspaper *Republika*. It was expected that Rahardjo would be appointed editor-in-chief. The position went instead, however, to a man with close ties to the then minister of information, Harmoko, a notorious Suharto crony.

A similar pattern of co-optation and control was repeated again and again over the next four years. As it became apparent that ICMI benefited from unqualified presidential favor, the organization was flooded with influence-seeking bureaucrats. By 1994–95, state bureaucrats so thoroughly dominated ICMI's leadership that independent Muslims complained bitterly that they had lost control of their own association.

Although severely circumscribed, the government's opening to Muslims nonetheless provided Muslim reformers with a platform for political discussion. Independents in the organization worked hard to sponsor seminars on human rights, economic reform, and constitutional law. Members of MASIKA, the youth wing of ICMI, were unceasing in their criticisms of corruption and their calls for democratic reform. Equally important, the government agreed to the establishment of an Islamic newspaper, after an almost 20-year absence, granting a general publication license (SIUPP) to ICMI in 1992. Its creation was welcomed even by those who understood that its editors would be subjected to intense political pressures. Between 1992 and 1998, the editors were repeatedly subjected to just such pressures. But political reformers on the staff continued to raise important questions. The ICMI-linked newsweekly, *Ummat*, was an even more consistent voice for change. It regularly carried stories critical of the government and calling for democratic reform. As the economy declined after August 1997, *Ummat* was in the forefront of presidential critics; in late 1997, it was among the first magazines to demand that the president resign.

These events indicate that the voices of political reform in ICMI and the Muslim community as a whole have always included a broader array of people than the restricted ranks of theological liberals and neomodernists. It is important to emphasize this point, because some Western observers have expressed the fear that the only Indonesian Muslims seriously committed to democratic reform have been theological liberals, and their numbers are small. In fact, however, the commitment to democracy and the rule of law is much broader.

Well known for his commitment to constitutional government and press freedoms, Sri Bintang Pamungkas, the legislator and ICMI member imprisoned by the government in 1996 for criticizing the president, has never been a neomodernist or theological liberal. A populist or even radical democrat in matters of politics—one who did not shy away, for example, from calling for the release of left-wing as well as Muslim political prisoners—Sri Bintang is known to be quite strict on theological matters. *Republika*'s business editor, Haidar Bagir, is similarly renowned for his principled commitment to journalistic integrity and intellectual freedom. Before coming to *Republika*, he demonstrated these virtues through his work at Mizan Press, one of the most remarkable publishers of political and religious literature in the Muslim world. Despite his liberalism as a publisher, on matters of worship and religious principle Haidar is also known to be strict.

Similarly, Amien Rais, the outspoken leader of the largest of Indonesia's reformist organizations, Muhammadiyah, is on theological matters also a rather strict constructionist. He has long made it clear that he is uncomfortable with the liberalized interpretations of Islam presented by such neomodernists as Nurcholish Madjid and Abdurrahman Wahid. Whatever his theological preference, Rais has a sophisticated understanding of democratic theory, and his support for press freedom, an independent judiciary, and free elections is sincere. As these and other examples illustrate, the commitment to political reform among ICMI independents, and in the Muslim leadership generally, is not restricted to theological liberals but is shared by a broad segment of the independent Muslim community.

After 1994, however, it was clear that the political opening (*keterbukaan*) trumpeted in the early 1990s had effectively come to a close. The banning of three of Indonesia's most respected newsweeklies in June 1994,[38] the trial and imprisonment of Sri Bintang Pamungkas in 1995–96, and the violent ouster of Megawati Sukarnoputri in July 1996 from the leadership of the Indonesian Democratic Party shocked those who hoped that Suharto was relaxing his hold on political affairs. Corruption scandals in the nation's supreme court, a crackdown on a fledgling independent labor movement, and stricter controls on nongovernmental organizations only added to the sense of despair. So too did the shameless abuses of the president's children, whose avarice was exceeded only by their indifference to the popular resentment they inspired.

All of these events had a decisive impact on the constellation of political forces of which Indonesian Muslims were part. In what follows, I want to look at the changing nature of these alliances by briefly examining the "ethno-religious" riots of 1995 to 1997 and the collapse of the regime in their wake. The violence involved dozens of incidents, including numerous attacks on Chinese and the burning or destruction of more than 200 Christian churches. These incidents were more than spontaneous expressions of popular resentment. They were evidence of the growing loss of consensus on political matters among the New Order elite. They also illustrate the way in which some in the highest levels of the state sought to advance their political agenda by exacerbating tensions in society.

State Terror

The violence of 1995 to 1997 was preceded by another incident, the reelection of Abdurrahman Wahid in December 1994 to the leadership of the Nahdlatul Ulama. The election was a tumultuous event, in which government officials worked behind the scenes in an ultimately unsuccessful effort to force Wahid out. It has been widely and, I believe, credibly argued that the effort ultimately failed because key members of the Indonesian military hostile to Suharto's political strategies indicated they had no interest in seeing Wahid overthrown. Here was an early sign of growing disagreement among the elite.

The logic of Wahid's opposition to ICMI and his ties to the military are complex subjects in their own right. Given the military's dominance in political affairs, no public leader in Indonesia can afford to ignore the military; civilian organizations require some measure of military patronage to survive. Contrary to its portrayal in some Western analyses, however, the military that dominates Indonesian politics has never been a Latin American–style junta organized around the personality and ideology of a single caudillo. On the contrary, although the armed forces are united in believing they have the right to intervene in politics, the specific interventions different commanders make are often oriented to competing or contradictory interests. Organizationally, too, different military leaders are aligned with competing civilian organizations. In times of elite conflict, military factions may attempt to outflank their rivals by mobilizing these civilian constituencies.

From the time of ICMI's founding in 1990, Wahid was keenly aware of the depth of military opposition to the organization. Although over the years he has had cordial ties with many of the independent Muslims involved in ICMI's establishment (such as, most notably, Nurcholish

Madjid), Wahid made clear from the beginning that he was strongly opposed to the organization. Despite a personal appeal by B. J. Habibie in the months following ICMI's founding, Wahid continued to make what are, by the standards of Indonesian politics, unusually harsh criticisms of the organization, denouncing it as sectarian and a refuge for Islamic fundamentalists. Although Wahid was aware of military opposition to ICMI, this was but one of the considerations influencing his uncompromising statements. In private discussions with friends in the pro-democracy discussion group Forum Democracy (of which he was the titular leader), Wahid also indicated that he feared that Suharto had established ICMI not merely to counter his opponents in the military but to divide the pro-democracy movement along religious lines. There is little doubt that this assessment of Suharto's intentions is correct, but the broad brush strokes of Wahid's criticisms led many in ICMI to argue that it was he, not they, who was fanning sectarian flames.

When the proposal to establish ICMI was first presented to the president in mid-1990, most high-ranking military officials, including Vice President Try Sutrisno, vigorously opposed it.[39] Weeks later, when it became clear that the president was intent on sponsoring the organization, most ceased their public criticisms. In a tried-and-true ploy of Indonesian politics, many military retirees even joined the organization. Nonetheless it was no secret that most high-ranking members of the military distrusted the organization and despised its flamboyant leader, Minister of Research and Technology B. J. Habibie.

Early on in his career, Habibie had been given control of the state-owned "strategic industries," including naval shipyards, an airplane construction factory, and armaments manufacture. This position gave him an enormous influence in budgetary matters, including those affecting the military. Military officials felt aggrieved when, in 1993, Habibie overruled their requests and arranged for the purchase of East German military vessels for the Indonesian Navy. The purchase was handled in a manner that circumvented normal military channels and saddled the military with vessels and rehabilitation expenses many officials felt were a drain on their budgets. The arrangement also ensured that Habibie was able to reap the benefits of the "management costs" associated with the purchase. In late 1993 and early 1994, the details of those management costs became the target of well-publicized press investigations. Although journalists involved in this reporting fiercely (and, I believe, credibly) deny that the military had anything to do with their inquiry, military officials clearly appreciated this light on Habibie's darker dealings; in private some expressed the hope that it might bring about his downfall. In June 1994, controversy caused by this investigative reporting provided the president with an excuse to shut down three of Indonesia's most distinguished newsmagazines, *Tempo, DeTik,* and *Editor.* The incident shocked domestic political observers and shattered hopes that Habibie might be a quiet advocate of political reform. The incident also signaled that Indonesia's brief flirtation with openness (*keterbukaan*) had come to an end.

A few months later, the campaign to remove Wahid from the NU leadership provided another indication of just how little remained of the promised era of openness. Who was behind the campaign? In elite Jakarta circles in 1995, the rumor was that there was a small dirty tricks bureau operating out of ICMI and that it was funneling money and logistical support to Wahid's enemies in NU. In interviews with me, ICMI officials repeatedly denied involvement in the campaign, although some made no effort to hide their dislike for Wahid. Although the issue was never raised in public, evidence provided to me by pro-democracy activists in ICMI opposed to the anti-Wahid campaign confirmed that the great majority of members in the organization knew nothing about the effort. However, this same information indicated that there was indeed a dirty tricks bureau coordinating the campaign against Wahid. According to these ICMI activists, the dirty tricks operation was run by a handful of people active in both ICMI and an intelligence bureau within the ruling party, Golkar. The fact that pro-democracy Muslims in ICMI brought this evidence to my attention illustrates that, contrary to some portrayals by Western scholars, ICMI has always been riven by internal dissent, and some among its membership have long sought to promote democratic decency.

Even though Wahid survived the assault on his leadership, the events surrounding the NU national congress in December 1994 worsened his relationship with ICMI. Wahid, too, was receiving intelligence briefings, and these indicated that there had been a campaign to unseat him and that it had been led by individuals operating out of a dirty tricks bureau linked to individuals in ICMI, Golkar, and a conservative Muslim think tank. Accurate or not, this evidence reminded Wahid that it was crucial that he maintain cordial ties to reform-minded members of the military, like those who had just helped him to retain his leadership post.

Wahid's relationship with ICMI continued to deteriorate during 1995 but took a decisive turn for the worse after the violent ouster of Megawati Sukarnoputri from the national headquarters of the Indonesian Democratic Party (PDI) on July 27, 1996. In the aftermath of this escalation in state violence, a report circulated among Wahid supporters and others in pro-democracy circles that the same dirty tricks bureau that had directed the campaign against Wahid had coordinated the campaign against Megawati. Megawati, the report said, was too *abangan* and too great a rival of Minister Habibie. As a show of loyalty to anti-Megawati forces in the government and in an effort to improve its influence with the president, this dirty tricks bureau agreed to coordinate the campaign for Megawati's overthrow. It must be emphasized once again that this was not an official ICMI campaign. But there is much evidence to suggest that individuals active in ICMI, Golkar, and a conservative Muslim think tank were indeed involved.

The intelligence reports reaching Wahid's supporters in the aftermath of the assault on the PDI put blame for the incident squarely on ICMI. The reports quickly became the subject of heated discussion among Wahid advisers, who saw the incident as one more illustration of the lengths to which his enemies were now willing to go. The fact that the individuals said to be responsible for the campaign happened to be nominally affiliated with ICMI made it easy for Wahid's supporters to blame the incident on the ICMI leadership as a whole. The available evidence suggests that this charge is too simple. ICMI has never been unitary in ideological or organizational terms. Its penetration early on by Suharto operatives rendered it all the more fissiparous. These details aside, Wahid came to the conclusion that, with Megawati out of the way, he was again the target of the dirty tricks bureau.

Against this backdrop of suspicion and violence, on October 10, 1996, fierce anti-Christian and anti-Chinese riots swept through the town of Situbondo in East Java, an NU stronghold. The riot stunned Wahid's supporters. Could their worst fears have been realized? Was this the event that many had forecast, intended to demonstrate that Wahid was a fraud, with little control over his supporters? Or was it, as Wahid's critics argued, merely an indication that Wahid was estranged from his rank and file, among whom there was growing resentment of Chinese and Christians?

As in the months prior to the September 30 coup in 1965, rumors often play a central role in Indonesian politics, and they can exercise a critical influence on political judgments. The reports circulating in NU circles after the Situbondo riots heightened anxieties among Wahid supporters. Many of the Situbondo rioters, field reports indicated, were not local people but provocateurs trucked in from outside town. Dressed in black uniforms, they had moved around town unimpeded, in a well-coordinated attack against churches and stores, all under the direction of whistle-blowing commanders.

Precisely who had organized this campaign remains unclear. Indonesian journalists, foreign reporters, and two eyewitnesses with whom I have spoken argue that the riots were not spontaneous. Shortly after the incident, even President Suharto commented that the violence had been orchestrated by a mysterious "third force" (he meant to give the impression, of course, that this force was really linked to the long-defunct Indonesian Communist Party). Among the security officials advising Wahid, the incident was taken as further proof that the dirty tricks bureau responsible for ousting Megawati was now honing in on Wahid and would use whatever means necessary to achieve its aim.

The cycle of violence had not yet ended. On the night of December 27, 1996, Indonesia was rocked by yet another riot. This incident took place in the West Java town of Tasikmalaya and involved attacks on churches, Chinese stores, and Chinese residences. Although not a NU stronghold, Tasikmalaya is regarded as a "*santri* [pious Muslim] city," and several of the youths arrested and charged with leading the riots happened to be members of NU's student organization. Once again, Wahid supporters were informed by security advisers that the riot had been orchestrated by anti-Wahid agents with ties to a secret bureau in ICMI. These reports alleged that the NU youths accused of leading the riots were affiliated with a pro-democracy organization that had been infiltrated by dirty tricks operatives; the operatives had then encouraged the membership to engage in violent protest. Shortly after learning of these reports, Wahid went public with his accusation that individuals linked to ICMI and a Muslim think tank were responsible for both the Situbondo and Tasikmalaya violence. What Wahid did not mention in his public accusation was that his same intelligence information indicated that renegade officers in the armed forces, linked to then Major-General Prabowo Subianto (President Suharto's son-in-law), were also alleged to have provided extensive logistical support to the rioters.

Muslim Resistance

This was the background to the astonishing political reconfiguration that emerged during the first half of 1997 in the run-up to May's national elections. The most extraordinary event in this reconfiguration was Abdurrahman Wahid's temporary withdrawal of support from the ousted leader of the Indonesian Democratic Party, Megawati Sukarnoputri, and his none-too-subtle expressions of support for the president and the government party, Golkar. For members of the democratic opposition, Wahid's public statements took on an even more bizarre air when Wahid made several well-publicized trips around the country in the company of the president's daughter Siti Hardiyanti Rukmana, the head of the Central and East Java branches of Golkar.

Wahid's actions were greeted in pro-democracy circles with a mix of resignation and anger. Wahid's defenders insisted he had no choice; events had forced him to put aside his democratic engagements so as to protect his NU base. If he failed to secure that base, they argued, he had no political future. Those less generous in their criticisms, including many reform-minded modernists, insisted that Wahid's democratic credentials had always been weak and that he had always worked to promote his own narrow interests. The alliance with the Suharto family only made this opportunism more apparent.

Events in the final months of 1997, however, demonstrated that the latter interpretation was simplistic. When Indonesia's economic crisis escalated in August and September of 1997, Wahid moved quickly to place himself at the forefront of those demanding reform. Friends of Wahid say he was determined to clear his name and correct the impression that he had bolted from the pro-democracy camp. Having moved earlier in the year to mend his relationship with Megawati, in September and October he met with her to demand the president initiate far-reaching economic reforms. In December 1997, just before his debilitating stroke (which he survived, but which sidelined him from political events during the first half of 1998), he joined with Megawati in what was, by the standards of Indonesian politics, an unprecedented move, openly calling for Suharto to step down. Indirectly, the campaign also aligned Wahid with Amien Rais, the outspoken leader of Indonesia's leading modernist organization, Muhammadiyah. In public, however, Wahid refused to consecrate the alliance with a formal declaration, maintaining the chill that has long marked his relationship with Rais.

During the first months of 1998, the campaign against Suharto hung perilously in balance. The Indonesian public seemed to hesitate in the face of enormous political uncertainties and the country's continuing economic decline. Student activists on campuses around the country continued to demand Suharto step down. In March, however, much of the public's attention shifted from the campus battles to Jakarta and the question of whether Suharto might satisfy calls for political change by appointing a reform cabinet. There was a widespread expectation that Suharto was to appoint Minister Habibie as vice president and at least a few ICMI reformists to his cabinet.

In the end, Habibie was appointed vice president. But in what can only be regarded as an astounding misstep, Suharto chose not to appoint any ICMI reformists to the cabinet, opting instead for cronies and uninspired loyalists. The slighting of ICMI pointed to what had become a growing tension in the Suharto camp. When they learned ICMI reformists might be included in the cabinet, several of Suharto's children reportedly lobbied their father to strike these names from his list. It was no secret that the president's children had an intense dislike of Habibie. Their dislike had intensified in late 1997, as they blamed Habibie for failing to control ICMI activists who joined the ranks of the pro-democracy movement. The president himself is said to have been angry at the Muslim media, especially *Ummat*, the ICMI-linked weekly that since mid-1997 had been at the forefront of those calling for democratic reform. In the end, Suharto went along with his children and excluded ICMI reformists from his cabinet.

This was a tactical blunder of enormous proportions. With this one action, Suharto galvanized Muslim opposition to his rule. With Wahid sidelined by a stroke and Megawati adopting a more retiring public role (a curious strategy that disappointed many of her followers), leadership of the anti-Suharto movement now passed into the hands of Amien Rais. Rais has long been regarded with suspicion by Indonesian secular nationalists. Leader of the 28-million-strong Muhammadiyah, Rais had been a founding member of ICMI. In 1997, however, he was expelled from ICMI's Board of Experts for his unceasing criticism of the first family's economic interests. Having been reprimanded by the president, however, Rais did not tone down his criticisms during 1997–98 but became only more outspoken.

Despite Rais's brave statements against Suharto, many secular democrats continued to regard him with suspicion. They remembered that, a few years earlier, Rais had made caustic statements concerning ethnic-Chinese Indonesians. On several occasions, he had also joined in attacks on government policies that, he claimed, had helped to Christianize segments of the Javanese population. Similarly, in the aftermath of the assault on the PDI headquarters in July 1996, Rais had condemned the government action but not rallied to the cause of the PDI itself. He is said to have regarded many PDI activists as too secular and too left-wing.

During 1997–98, however, the political crisis gave Rais his first opportunity to act as a true national leader, not merely the head of a Muslim social organization. He responded to the challenge with courage and skill. In early 1998, it was Rais who called for an alliance with Wahid and Megawati against Suharto. Since Wahid's distrust of Rais is well known, Rais's appeal was indicative of his determination to put aside personal disagreements in the interest of the pro-democracy struggle. Rais told his advisers (among whom are Syafi'i Anwar and Syafi Maarif, two modernist intellectuals rightly renowned for their religious ecumenicism and democratic decency) that he realized that the movement could not win without a broader base. In this instance, however, it was Wahid who balked. Wahid declined to join formally with Rais because he thought Rais had not sufficiently distanced himself from those who wanted a more formal institutionalization of Islam in state and society.

By April 1998 it was clear that opposition to Suharto was again gaining momentum. At the same time, however, there was widespread anxiety among civilians and reformist members of the military that the president might be preparing to unleash fiercer violence. The well-publicized kidnapping and torture of student activists during the first months of 1998 suggested the escalation had indeed begun.

One figure in the Suharto camp caused pro-democracy Muslims particular concern. On the evening of January 23, 1998, during the Muslim fasting month, the president's son-in-law Lieutenant-General Prabowo Subianto met to break the fast with several hundred supporters of the conservative Islamist leader Ahmad Soemargono. A little-known figure prior to 1994, Soemargono had ties to the conservative-modernist DDII. In the late 1980s, Soemargono had developed an activist organization of his own (still strongly linked to DDII) known by its acronym KISDI, the Indonesian Committee for Solidarity with the Islamic World. The rapidity of Soemargono's rise surprised Muslim politicians, who were not used to seeing unfamiliar figures achieve such prominence without the backing of an established Muslim organization. Many suspected Soemargono might have a secret benefactor. Soemargono also raised eyebrows because his public statements against Christians, Chinese, the United States, and other "enemies of Islam" were out of character with the Indonesian Muslim mainstream. Equally serious, Soemargono did not limit his diatribes to non-Muslims. After the bloody attack on Megawati's PDI in 1996, Soemargono was at the forefront of the conservative Islamists attacking Muslim intellectuals who had criticized the government. Such people, Soemargono said, were "procommunist" and "anti-Islamic." The most consistent target of Soemargono's wrath was the ICMI newspaper *Republika*.[40]

Among ICMI reformists and pro-democracy Muslims, it was widely rumored that Soemargono's rise had been aided by the man with whom he broke the fast that January evening, Lieutenant-General Prabowo. Prabowo had been cultivating ties among Muslim politicians since the late 1980s. Well known for his obsessive hatred of the Catholic general Benny Murdani, in meetings with Muslim activists Prabowo spoke openly of the need to free Indonesia of "minority tyranny." These statements, and Prabowo's volatile personality, alarmed Muslim moderates. With its strident calls for the government to take action against the Chinese and other "enemies of Islam," the January meeting of Prabowo and Soemargono heightened their sense of alarm.

After the public ceremony with the KISDI activists, Prabowo met privately with a smaller number of conservative Muslim leaders. In that meeting, he is said to have provided them with documents that purported to explain the logic of Indonesia's economic crisis and the country's ongoing negotiations with the International Monetary Fund (IMF).[41] The documents painted a picture of a vile conspiracy against Suharto. The IMF, the United States, Israel, and Indonesia's pro-democracy movement were all united in a giant "Jewish-Jesuit-American-Chinese" effort to topple Suharto. The reasons President Suharto had been targeted, the documents explained, were that he was a Muslim and that he and his family were becoming too powerful for the cabal of Jews, Jesuits, Chinese, and CIA-Mossad agents who control world capitalism. Among the many other outrageous details provided in these documents was the charge that the death of the president's wife, Tien, the year prior was not a natural event. On the contrary, the documents explained, Tien had been murdered by a Chinese doctor who had deliberately misled the president by giving her a clean bill of health just a day before she died. She had been killed on the instruction of Christians and secular-nationalists in the government intent on eliminating the first lady and then the president, all as a prelude to seizing control of the state.

These bizarre allegations help to explain a number of events that occurred at the margins of the pro-democracy struggle in February and March 1998. In late January, a bomb went off in central Jakarta; its fabricator escaped. At the site of the bomb blast, however, police found a rather unusual document: an e-mail message purported to be from one of Indonesia's wealthiest Chinese businessmen, Sofyan Wanandi. Wanandi has long been benefactor of the Center for Strategic and International Studies (CSIS), a conservative think tank once linked to Suharto but now in opposition. It retained close ties, however, with General Murdani. The alleged e-mail message was from Wanandi to the small People's Democratic Party (PRD), a leftist organization that had been blamed by the government for the riots that followed the assault on the PDI in July 1996. The message explained that Wanandi was prepared to give the PRD funds for a bombing campaign to bring the Suharto government down. The agreement described in the document between a conservative Chinese millionaire and a small band of left-wing radicals is so implausible as to be laughable. But the message's political intent was all too apparent. The economic crisis shaking Indonesia is not the result of presidential cronyism or corruption, it implied, but a campaign financed by ungrateful Chinese and hateful pro-democracy activists.

For a few days, a number of conservative Islamists attempted to rally to this call. Lukman Harun, a high-ranking official in Muhammadiyah (and an enemy of Amien Rais), responded to the charge by calling for a campaign, not against Suharto, but against all "rats" and "traitors" to the nation. To whom might this inflammatory statement apply? Lukman went on to say that Suharto is the leader not only of Indonesia but of all Indonesian Muslims. The gauntlet for an assault on Chinese, Christian, and pro-democracy challengers to the regime was thrown down.

The evidence indicates that these and other desperate measures to save the Suharto regime were engineered by his son-in-law Lieutenant-General Prabowo. What is more remarkable, however, is that these initiatives not only failed, but they hardened pro-democracy Muslims' opposition to Suharto. During my visit to Jakarta in March 1998, an ICMI intellectual who attended the Soemargono meeting with Prabowo in January told me he was so alarmed by what he had witnessed that he immediately reported it to his colleagues, alerting them to this escalation in Prabowo provocations. Nurcholish Madjid, Amien Rais, and *Ummat* responded not by toning down their calls for peaceful reformation but by intensifying them.

In Suharto's final days, Prabowo repeatedly threatened violence against Suharto's enemies. Many suspect that he was responsible for the killing of the four students at the Trisakti University in Jakarta on May 12. Many also believe that he was involved in organizing some of the worst incidents of theft, rape, and murder directed against Chinese Indonesians during the awful riots of May 13–15. Shortly after the riots, Prabowo's aides are alleged to have warned Amien Rais that he would turn Independence Square in central Jakarta into a "sea of blood" if Amien went ahead with his planned demonstration against the president on May 20.[42] In the early hours of that day Rais called off the event after traveling to Independence Square and realizing Prabowo had indeed positioned troops in full battle gear to block the event.

Evidence provided me by pro-democracy Muslims also indicates that Prabowo provided the directives and funding for a KISDI rally of conservative Muslims against pro-democracy activists at the National Assembly on May 22. By the time Prabowo was able to stage this event, of course, it was too late to save Suharto, since he had resigned the preceding day. The KISDI organizers nonetheless went ahead with the demonstration. They changed its theme from a defense of Suharto to a rally for the new president, B. J. Habibie. Some of the banners carried at the event indicated the new KISDI emphasis, "Opposition to Habibie = Opposition to Islam." "Never have I ever been more ashamed," one ICMI reformist told me, "than when I saw those demonstrators abusing the brave pro-democracy students, so many of whom are Muslims, in the name of Islam."

Conclusion: Indonesia in the Balance

As this overview of events indicates, 20 years of Islamic resurgence have not created a Muslim political consensus. Nor have those years united Muslims around a common leader. But it is important to recognize this much in Muslim Indonesian politics: years of struggle against Suharto's dictatorship deepened the mainstream's commitment to democracy, constitutional law, civil independence, and peaceful reformation. Whatever the outcome of Indonesia's current crisis, the actions of Nurcholish Madjid, Amien Rais, Dawam Rahardjo, Abdurrahman Wahid, and other mainstream Muslims were a model of political courage and democratic principle. In the face of violent repression, these leaders held firmly to their calls for "Reformasi Damai" (Peaceful Reformation). In the face of Lieutenant-General Prabowo's ham-fisted efforts to cloak the president in the garb of Islam, all but a few ultra-conservatives rejected this vile abuse of their religion and demanded the president step down.

This is not to say that the road to democracy or a consensus on just what Indonesian democracy should be is going to be reached any time soon. An economic crisis of the proportions into which Indonesia is now falling would strain the political confidence of the most settled democracies. Although Suharto has resigned, his family and supporters still wield great power. Despite the working alliances established in the campaign against Suharto, there is still a bitter divide between political reformers committed to a secular or (more precisely) "nonconfessional" nationalism, such as Wahid and most of the military, and those who would give a more Islamic cast to Indonesian democracy. This tension will animate Indonesian politics for years to come.

Although Wahid and Rais have both pointed their organizations in the direction of democracy and the rule of law, each confronts daunting challenges. Health problems will handicap Wahid. While many urban *ulama* and youth leaders endorse Wahid's views, NU's rank and file are more cautious than this avant-garde. At this point, too, none among Wahid's potential successors commands the personal charisma necessary to maintain the loyalty of mainstream *ulama*. If Wahid disappears, therefore, NU's influence and its leadership's commitment to a nonconfessional nationalism may diminish somewhat. But there is no reason to fear an abrupt change of course.

At the time of this writing (July 1998), Wahid has also expressed the intention of forging an alliance with secular nationalists in Megawati's Indonesian Democratic Party. He has made clear that this would be his alliance, not a formal union of Megawati and NU. If this alliance moves forward, it is likely that it will be a major player in the national elections. However, it is also likely that a significant proportion of the NU rank and file would opt not to follow Wahid, saving their vote for a more explicitly Islamic party. NU's heretofore remarkable ability to maintain its electoral base, so visible in the elections of 1955 and 1971, may well be diminished.

Rais and the Muslim modernists confront equally daunting challenges. Although from mid-1997 to mid-1998 Rais made repeated attempts to expand his base and present himself as a leader for all Indonesians, he is still regarded with suspicion by secular democrats, traditionalist Muslims, and at least some Muslim liberals. Already, during trips to East Java in June 1998, he was greeted with fierce demonstrations by NU supporters intent on indicating that his vision of democratic Islam was not theirs. An equally serious difficulty for Rais is that his base constituency, the modernist Muslim community, is deeply divided. Conservatives aligned with Soemargono's KISDI and the hard-line faction of the DDII are not numerous, but their ideological fervor and organizational discipline give them a power in excess of their numbers. They have already indicated that they disagree with Rais's efforts to extend his pro-democracy alliance across religious and ethnic lines. They want a neo-Masyumi party pure and simple—and one that would be considerably more conservative than the Masyumi of the early 1950s. It seems likely that such a conservative party would not be among the top vote getters in national elections and that Rais and other moderates will continue to command the respect of the modernist mainstream. But the ultraconservative fringe will continue to operate, forming its own parties and fragmenting the modernist vote. The possibility also exists that if Indonesia's crisis worsens—and if renegade elements of the political elite again resort to ethno-religious violence to get their way—a small number of ultraconservatives may be willing to be drawn into extraconstitutional initiatives. (Indeed, the threats of violence against Chinese seen in spray-painted graffiti in towns across Indonesia during June and July 1998 suggest that some such extremists are still active and are as intent as ever on driving Sino-Indonesian citizens out of Indonesia.) But such extremism will be fiercely opposed among the Muslim mainstream.

In short, post-Suharto Indonesia is unlikely to see a single, dominant Islamic grouping any time soon; it is even less likely to see a clear Muslim consensus on the role of Islam in the state. There will likely be several conservative Islamist parties, a larger and thoroughly moderate Muhammadiyah-linked party, one or several NU parties, and, possibly, a "rainbow" coalition linking Megawati supporters and Abdurrahman Wahid. Under these circumstances, the divide between modernist and neotraditionalist Islam will remain a conspicuous feature of the Indonesian political landscape. Far more than in the 1950s, however, this divide will now be complicated by the presence of conservative Islamists and, more significantly, pious Muslims committed to a more-or-less secular nationalism.

Two variables introduce additional uncertainty into this already complicated scene: the economic crisis and the attitude of the military. Since the military is the subject of another chapter in this volume, suffice it to say here that all evidence indicates that the generals are divided on the question of Islam but not irreparably so. The central leadership remains committed to a pluralist-Pancasila Indonesia. However, by comparison with the military of the early 1980s, they are also willing to accept a greater Islamic presence in society. A small but dedicated minority among the generals might wish to encourage a deeper Islamization of state and society. Although his misdeeds are not representative of the group as a whole, however, Prabowo has done enormous damage to the Muslim generals' cause. The majority of high-ranking officers have felt their convictions confirmed that although Islam may be given special recognition in public affairs, there must be no serious tampering with the multiconfessional basis of the state.

The depression into which Indonesia is now sinking will exacerbate the ethno-religious imbalance between Chinese and indigenous (*pribumi*) Indonesians. Since the early 1980s, the ultraconservative wing of the Dewan Dakwah Islamiyah Indonesia has been unstinting in its critiques of the "Christianization" of Indonesian society. For this group, this dastardly scheme has in part succeeded owing to Chinese economic dominance. There can be no question that the basic premises of this argument—that the Chinese have enjoyed unfair economic advantages and used these to promote Christianity—fall on sympathetic ears among a segment of the urban poor and middle class. Although the majority of Muslims reject conspiracy theories, most also feel that some kind of affirmative action program is needed for the Muslim poor.

The situation is complex, however, and any economic settlement will depend strongly on the military and the Indonesian economy itself. Although the military has a few economic nationalists resentful of Chinese influence, the majority are wary of too-radical efforts to transform the economy. In addition, in the present economic crisis, it is clear the state lacks the resources to carry out even a modest version of the New Economic Policy conducted in Malaysia from 1971 to 1996. A bitter lesson it will be—but the economic crisis may deepen the conviction that excessive meddling in the market at this point only alienates investors (domestic and foreign) and delays Indonesia's recovery.

Thus the political future of Indonesian Islam remains clouded. The economic crisis will worsen the plight of the urban underclass, the overwhelming majority of whom are Muslim. In these circumstances, the future seems certain to keep the divide between Christian-Chinese "haves" and Muslim "have-nots" very much in the public eye. Inasmuch as this is so, we should not be surprised to see continued sniping between Muslim moderates and liberals, on one side, and rivals demanding a greater "Islamization" of the state and economy.

The outcome of this conflict will depend greatly on the policies of Suharto's successors. Indonesia's tradition of religious pluralism and tolerance can survive, and the democratic commitments so courageously demonstrated in the actions of pro-democracy students and Muslims can become a sustainable resource for democratic reform. Now more than ever, however, the achievement of these objectives will depend upon the military and civilian leadership's grasp of two lessons from the struggle against the Suharto dictatorship. The first is that the Muslim community's (and everyone else's) sense of participation in the political process must be decisively heightened, so that it becomes easier to discredit those unscrupulous actors who would go outside the law and use the labels of Islam (or "anti-Islam") for their own narrow gain. The second lesson is that Muslim and other Indonesian leaders must work hard to socialize the awareness that the pluralism and compromise so visible in the pro-democracy struggle were not just momentary concessions on the road to political triumph but are democracy's most trying, but essential, requirements.

In any society, let alone one confronting one of the most severe economic crises of the late 20th century, these would be difficult lessons to apply. But Indonesian democrats, Muslim and non-Muslim, have just shown themselves capable of rising to great challenges. In coming months there will be struggles and setbacks, but there are grounds for hope.

Notes

1. See, for example, Samuel Huntington's unitary portrayal of Islam in *The Clash of Civilizations and the Remaking of World Order* (New York: Simon & Schuster, 1996).

2. Dale F. Eickelman and James Piscatori, *Muslim Politics* (Princeton: Princeton University Press, 1996, p. 5).
3. Benedict Anderson, *Imagined Communities: Reflections on the Origin and Spread of Nationalism* (London: Verso, 1983).
4. On the influence of media and publishing on the Islamic revival around the world, see, among others, G. N. Atiyeh, "The Book in the Modern Arab World: The Cases of Lebanon and Egypt," in *The Book in the Islamic World: The Written Word and Communication in the Middle East,* ed. G. N. Atiyeh (Albany: State University of New York Press, 1995), pp. 232–53; Dale F. Eickelman, "Islamic Liberalism Strikes Back," *Middle East Studies Association Bulletin* 27 (1993): 163–68; and Robert W. Hefner, "Print Islam: Mass Media and Ideological Rivalries in Indonesian Islam," *Indonesia* 64 (October 1997): 77–103.
5. On populist preachers in contemporary Islam, see Richard T. Antoun, *Muslim Preacher in the Modern World: A Jordanian Case Study in Comparative Perspective* (Princeton: Princeton University Press, 1989); and Patrick D. Gaffney, *The Prophet's Pulpit: Islamic Preaching in Contemporary Egypt* (Berkeley: University of California Press, 1994). On the role of neotraditionalist Sufis in Muslim social movements, see R. Launay, *Beyond the Stream: Islam and Society in a West African Town* (Berkeley: University of California Press, 1992); Serif Mardin, "Civil Society and Islam," in *Civil Society: Theory, History, Comparison,* ed. J. A. Hall (London: Polity, 1995), pp. 278–300; and L. A. Villalon, *Islamic Society and State Power in Senegal: Disciples and Citizens in Fatick* (Cambridge: Cambridge University Press, 1995). On secularly educated new Muslim intellectuals, see Michael E. Meeker, "The New Muslim Intellectuals in the Republic of Turkey," in *Islam in Modern Turkey: Religion, Politics and Literature in a Secular State,* ed. R. Tapper (London: I.B. Tauris & Co., 1991), pp. 189–219; and Olivier Roy, *The Failure of Political Islam,* trans. Carol Volk (Cambridge: Harvard University Press, 1994).
6. Eickelman and Piscatori, *Muslim Politics,* p. 71.
7. For examples of how this fragmentation may promote democratization, see Villalon, *Islamic Society and State Power;* and Robert W. Hefner, "Introduction," in *Islam in an Era of Nation-States: Politics and Religious Renewal in Muslim Southeast Asia,* ed. Robert N. Hefner and Patricia Horvatich (Honolulu: University of Hawaii Press, 1997), pp. 3–40.
8. For tragic examples, see G. E. Fuller, *Algeria: The Next Fundamentalist State?* (Santa Monica: RAND, 1996); and Roy, *The Failure of Political Islam.*
9. Gavin W. Jones and Chris Manning, "Labour Force and Employment during the 1980s," in *The Oil Boom and After: Indonesian Economic Policy and Performance in the Soeharto Era,* ed. Anne Booth (Kuala Lumpur: Oxford University Press, 1992), pp. 363–410.

10. Terence H. Hull and Gavin W. Jones, "Demographic Perspectives," in *Indonesia's New Order: The Dynamics of Socio-Economic Transformation*, ed. Hal Hill (Honolulu: University of Hawaii Press, 1994), pp. 123–78.
11. Robert Wuthnow, *The Restructuring of American Religion* (Princeton: Princeton University Press, 1988).
12. See Robert W. Hefner, *Hindu Javanese: Tengger Tradition and Islam* (Princeton: Princeton University Press, 1985), and "Islamizing Java? Religion and Politics in Rural East Java," *Journal of Asian Studies* 46, no. 3 (1987): 533–54. For an in-depth study of a similar process of Islamization in rural Central Java, see M. Bambang Pranowo, "Creating Islamic Traditions in Rural Java," (Melbourne, Australia: Ph.D. Dissertation, Department of Anthropology and Sociology, Monash University, 1991).
13. For Sumatran examples, see John R. Bowen, *Muslims through Discourse: Religion and Ritual in Gayo Society* (Princeton: Princeton University Press, 1993); and Rita Smith Kipp, *Dissociated Identities: Ethnicity, Religion, and Class in an Indonesian Society* (Ann Arbor: University of Michigan Press, 1993); for rural East Java, see Robert W. Hefner, *The Political Economy of Mountain Java: An Interpretive History* (Berkeley: University of California Press, 1990).
14. Adam Schwarz, *A Nation in Waiting: Indonesia in the 1990s* (Boulder: Westview, 1994), p. 164.
15. Andrée Feillard, *Islam et armée dans l'Indonésie contemporaine* (Paris: L'Harmattan, 1995), pp. 146–50.
16. On government restrictions on business associations, see Andrew MacIntyre, *Business and Politics in Indonesia* (Sydney: Allen & Unwin, 1990).
17. Among many fine anthropological studies of conversion in the face of New Order religious policies, see Lorraine V. Aragon, "Revised Rituals in Central Sulawesi: The Maintenance of Traditional Cosmological Concepts in the Face of Allegiance to World Religion," *Anthropological Forum* 6, no. 3 (1992): 371–84; Jane Atkinson, "Religions in Dialogue: The Construction of an Indonesian Minority Religion," American Ethnologist 10, no. 4 (1983): 684–96; Janet Hoskins, "Entering the Bitter House: Spirit Worship and Conversion in West Sumba," in *Indonesian Religions in Transition*, ed. Rita Smith Kipp and Susan Rodgers (Tucson: University of Arizona Press, 1987), pp. 136–60; Rita Smith Kipp, *Dissociated Identities;* Martin Rossler, "Islamization and the Reshaping of Identities in Rural South Sulawesi," in *Islam in an Era of Nation-States*, ed. Hefner and Horvatich pp. 275–306; and Patricia Spyer, "Serial Conversion/Conversion to Seriality: Religion, State, and Number in Aru, Eastern Indonesia," in *Conversion to Modernities: The Globalization of Christianity*, ed. P. van der Veer (London: Routledge, 1996), pp. 171–98.
18. Examples of explicitly anti-Islamic new religious movements in Java can be found in Clifford Geertz, "Ritual and Social Change: A Javanese Exam-

ple," in *The Interpretation of Cultures,* ed. Clifford Geertz (New York: Basic Books, 1973), pp. 142–169; and in Hefner, "Islamizing Java?"

19. The best discussion of the fate of Javanist mysticism in the early New Order is Paul Stange, "The Sumarah Movement in Javanese Mysticism" (Madison, Wisconsin: Ph.D. Dissertation, Department of History, University of Wisconsin, 1980), and his "'Legitimate' Mysticism in Indonesia," *Review of Indonesian and Malaysian Affairs* 20, no. 2 (1986): 76–117. Sven Cederroth, *Survival and Profit in Rural Java: The Case of an East Javanese Village* (London: Curzon, 1995), provides a more recent, and somewhat more optimistic, case study from rural East Java. It is important to add here that, notwithstanding the Islamic revival of the 1980s and 1990s, *kepercayaan* mysticism is far from spent as a cultural force, and disputes over its role in Indonesian society will figure in debates over state religious policies for years to come.
20. Examples of this privatization of previously public village traditions can be seen in Cederroth, *Survival and Profit;* Pranowo, "Creating Islamic Traditions"; and Robert W. Hefner, "Of Faith and Commitment: Christian Conversion in Muslim Java," in *Conversion to Christianity: Historical and Anthropological Perspectives on a Great Transformation,* ed. Robert W. Hefner (Berkeley and London: University of California Press, 1993), pp. 99–125.
21. For detailed discussions of the killings in Java, see the essays in ed. Robert Cribb, *The Indonesian Killings: Studies from Java and Bali* (Clayton, Victoria: Center for Southeast Asian Studies, Monash University, 1990); and Hefner, *The Political Economy of Mountain Java,* pp. 193–227.
22. On the politics and culture of diversion from Islam, see Hyung-Jun Kim, "Reformist Muslims in a Yogyakarta Village" (Canberra: Ph.D. Dissertation, Department of Anthropology, Australian National University, 1996); and Margaret L. Lyon, "Politics and Religious Identity: Genesis of a Javanese-Hindu Movement in Rural Central Java" (Berkeley: Ph.D. Dissertation, Department of Anthropology, University of California, 1977).
23. For an excellent discussion of the reception of democratic ideals among Indonesian Muslim intellectuals, see Masykuri Abdillah, *Responses of Indonesian Muslim Intellectuals to the Concept of Democracy (1966–1993)* (Hamburg: Abera Verlag Meyer & Co., 1997).
24. See Roy, *The Failure of Political Islam,* pp. 89–106.
25. On NU's history and organization, see Andrée Feillard, *Islam et armée* and Martin van Bruinessen, *NU: Tradisi, Relasi-relasi Kuasa, Pencarian Wacana Baru* [NU: Tradition, power relations, and the search for a new discourse] (Yogyakarta: LKiS, 1994).
26. Feillard, *Islam et armée;* and Martin van Bruinessen, *Rakyat Kecil, Islam dan Politik* [The people, Islam, and politics] (Yogyakarta: Bentang Budaya, 1998).
27. See the discussion of NU's effort to develop a banking system in the early 1990s in Robert W. Hefner, "Islamizing Capitalism: On the Founding of

Indonesia's First Islamic Bank," in *Toward a New Paradigm: Recent Developments in Indonesian Islamic Thought*, ed. Mark Woodward (Tempe: Center for Southeast Asian Studies, Arizona State University, 1996), pp. 291–322.

28. M. Syafi'i Anwar, *Pemikiran dan Aksi Islam Indonesia: Sebuah Kajian Politik Tentang Cendekiawan Muslim Orde Baru* [The thought and action of Indonesian Islam: A political study of New Order Muslim intellectuals] (Jakarta: Paramadina, 1995); Muhammad Kamal Hassan, *Muslim Intellectual Responses to "New Order" Indonesia* (Kuala Lumpur: Dewan Bahasa dan Pustaka Madjid, 1980); Nurcholish Madjid, *Islam, Kemodernan, dan Ke-Indonesiaan* [Islam, modernity, and Indonesianness] (Bandung: Mizan, 1984), and "Islamic Roots of Modern Pluralism: Indonesian Experience," *Studia Islamika: Indonesian Journal for Islamic Studies* 1, no. 1 (1994): 55–77.

29. On the cultural logic of this strategy, see Greg Barton, "Neo-Modernism: A Vital Synthesis of Traditionalist and Modernist Islamic Thought in Indonesia," *Studia Islamika: Indonesian Journal for Islamic Studies* 2, no. 3 (1995): 1–71; Robert W. Hefner, "Islamization and Democratization in Indonesia," in *Islam in an Era of Nation States*, ed. Hefner and Horvatich, pp. 75–127; and Dedy Djamaluddin Malik and Idi Subandy Ibrahim, *Zaman Baru Islam Indonesia: Pemikiran dan Aksi Politik* [Indonesian Islam's new era: Ideas and political action] (Jakarta: Zaman Wacana Mulia, 1997).

30. Allan A. Samson, "Islam and Politics in Indonesia" (Berkeley: Ph.D. Dissertation, Department of Political Science, University of California, 1972).

31. On the relationship of Muslim entrepreneurs to New Order crony capitalism, see John Bresnan, *Managing Indonesia: The Modern Political Economy* (New York: Columbia University Press, 1993); Richard Robison, "Industrialization and the Economic and Political Development of Capital: The Case of Indonesia," in *Southeast Asian Capitalists*, ed. Ruth McVey (Ithaca: Southeast Asia Program, Cornell University, 1992), pp. 65–88; and Robert W. Hefner "Markets and Justice for Muslim Indonesians," in *Market Cultures: Society and Morality in the New Asian Capitalisms*, ed. Robert W. Hefner (Boulder: Westview, 1998), pp. 224–50.

32. On the DDII, see Hefner, "Print Islam."

33. This transformation from regime critic to supporter has been discussed in surprisingly frank terms in the DDII's publications. In a two-page statement released in its Internet edition on March 12, 1998 (another version of which appeared in the DDII journal *Media Dakwah*), the DDII editorial board wrote: "In the 1970s and the 1980s, Media Dakwah was the magazine most vigorously opposed to the Suharto government, because of policies that always marginalized the Muslim community. . . . But since the end of the 1980s, we recognized objectively that there had been a change in Suharto policies on matters affecting the Indonesian Muslim community. This doesn't mean we are not still critical toward the government. . . . [But] we do not want now to become drawn into a scenario to bring down a government that is legal and constitutional; at the same time

we know precisely that there are groups that up to now have been extremely anti-Islamic and are ready and willing to seize power."

34. This is not to say that democratic discussions in the non-Muslim and secular nationalist community did not figure in this exchange. On the contrary, non-Muslims and secular nationalists have often introduced ideas then drawn into Muslim discussions. Such writers as the human rights lawyer Todung Mulya Lubis (a Christian), Adnan Buyung Nasution (a practicing Muslim and distinguished advocate of nonconfessional democracy and the constitutional rule of law), and Marsillam Simanjuntak (a Christian and secular political theorist influenced by Jurgen Habermas's political ideas) were at the forefront of the movement for legal and democratic reform. But the dissemination of these writers' ideas to a broader Indonesian public ultimately depended on the receptivity of many in the Muslim community to democratic ideals.

35. For overviews of ICMI's founding, see Anwar, *Pemikiran dan Aksi,* and Hefner, "Islamization and Democratization."

36. See Schwarz, *A Nation in Waiting,* p. 187.

37. For an overview of government concessions to Islam, see Bahtiar Effendy, "Islam and the State: The Transformation of Islamic Political Ideas and Practices in Indonesia" (Columbus, Ohio: Ph.D. Dissertation, Department of Political Science, Ohio State University, 1994).

38. See the Human Rights Watch report, *The Limits of Openness: Human Rights in Indonesia and East Timor* (New York: Human Rights Watch, 1994).

39. See Hefner, "Islamization and Democratization," p. 104.

40. KISDI attacks on *Republika* are discussed in Hefner, "Print Islam."

41. I was given copies of these documents by a Muslim activist who attended the meeting and was shocked by the plans discussed there. The largest of the texts was a printed booklet of 56 pages entitled *Konspirasi mengguyang Soeharto* [The Conspiracy to Bring Down Suharto]. Portions of the document were subsequently circulated in conservative Islamist circles and published on the Internet.

42. This information was provided to me by an aide to Rais; I was unable to verify this claim with Amien Rais himself.

4

The Indonesian Military in Politics

TAKASHI SHIRAISHI

THE RESIGNATION of President Suharto on May 21, 1998, brought an abrupt end to Indonesia's 32-year-old New Order regime and started the process of redrawing the country's political map. The military, as the most powerful political institution in Suharto's Indonesia, came under immediate pressure to scale back its political role.

A number of leading civilian politicians demanded a review of the military's cherished dual-function doctrine, which gives the armed forces a major social and political role in addition to its security function. Others campaigned for the military to return to the barracks immediately and relinquish its political responsibilities. Even reformist leaders within the armed forces—which are known as ABRI—conceded that a redefinition of *dwifungsi,* as the dual-function doctrine is called, was overdue. Privately, some senior military figures acknowledge that the military's day-to-day role in politics is almost certain to decline over the medium term, and perhaps disappear altogether.

Clearly, as of this writing in August 1998, the military was on the defensive. One of its rising stars, Lieutenant-General Prabowo Subianto, had been discharged from the military for his involvement in the abduction and disappearance of pro-democracy activists earlier in the year; a formal court-martial was still being considered. The military was under attack for a series of human rights violations during the New Order period, up to and including the last months of Suharto's rule. Many civilian politicians blamed the military for participating in, or facilitating, some of the worst excesses of Suharto's rule.

But even though its self-image as the irreplaceable backbone of the nation had been badly tarnished, the military retains considerable political clout. An abandonment of the dual-function doctrine and a return to the barracks are highly unlikely in the near term. The weakness of civilian political parties, the erosion of political institutions under Suharto's rule, the transitional nature of President B. J. Habibie's administration, and the threats to law and order presented by the ongoing economic crisis all indicate a continued and substantial political influence for the armed forces in the next few years.

Exactly how much influence the military will cede, and in what areas, is too soon to say. I will return to its future later in the chapter. First, though, I want to begin with a discussion of the military's role in the final days of the New Order and of the political dynamics within the military leadership in recent years.

Structural Power

Before Suharto stepped down, many in and outside Indonesia had talked of military intervention as a way of breaking the political impasse. In its February 21, 1998, issue, the British magazine the *Economist* went so far as to make a not-too-subtle call for a coup. Political observers speculated on scenarios that borrowed from the 1988 coup in Burma, the transfer of presidential powers from former Indonesian President Sukarno to Suharto in 1966, the student revolution in Thailand in 1973, and the 1986 military revolt in the Philippines.

In the end, the Indonesian military did play a role in bringing the New Order to an end, although it did not directly intervene. ABRI leaders never directly told Suharto to stand down. Nevertheless, the struggle within the upper echelons of the military had a powerful influence on the political process and on events in the country more generally. For example, General Wiranto, the commander-in-chief of the armed forces, and his military allies played an important role in Suharto's decision to step down by giving student-led demonstrators relatively wide latitude.

Similarly, at least for now, no coup is brewing against Habibie's transitional government. As in the past, the military remains reluctant to seize political control unless circumstances outside its ranks force its hand. At the same time, no government in Indonesia can survive for long without the military's support, and the current senior officers seem satisfied with that measure of power.

The military, with the army as its backbone, possesses what can be called structural power, resulting from its monopoly on state coercive power, its institutionalized role in the political process, its domination of Indonesia's intelligence community, and its reach all the way down to the village level. Further, the military has the capability to take over state power, provided it is able to form a consensus within its top ranks to do so.

The Indonesian military consists of three services—the army, the navy, and the air force—plus the national police, with a combined force strength of half a million, of which 240,000 are army troops, 47,000 navy, 23,000 air force, and 190,000 police.[1] It is headed by the commander-in-chief of the armed forces, who is supported by the two armed forces chiefs of staff—the chief of general staff and the chief of social and political staff—along with the three service chiefs of staff and the chief of national police. Its structure reflects its purpose: to maintain internal security and provide a framework for guerrilla and low-level conventional operations. It is not organized to mount a credible high-level conventional defense.

The military also has a say in national and local politics under the doctrine of dual function mentioned earlier. Indeed, its sociopolitical role expanded dramatically throughout the New Order. Military officers are allocated seats in the National Parliament and in the People's Consultative Assembly, an electoral body that meets once every five years to choose a president and vice president. Military officers also hold seats in provincial and district assemblies, and are seconded to nonmilitary posts in the government, serving as ambassadors, provincial governors, and district chiefs, as well as within the top ranks of the bureaucracy.[2] By the early-1990s, an estimated 14,000 military personnel held posts outside the formal military structure.

The military's control over the political process is facilitated by a comprehensive intelligence network. The Armed Forces Intelligence Agency (BIA), which reports directly to the commander-in-chief, dominates Indonesia's intelligence community.[3] In addition, the nonmilitary intelligence arms—such as the State Intelligence Coordinating Agency (BAKIN), which reports directly to the president; the Directorate-General for Social and Political Affairs at the Ministry of Interior; and the Office of the Deputy Attorney General for Intelligence—are all headed by military officers.

The army is the most powerful military service. Not only does the commander-in-chief of the armed forces always come from the army, but army officers dominate armed forces headquarters in Jakarta.[4] Of the 16 operational commands directly under the commander-in-chief, 12 are army commands. Moreover, army officers also have first call on the most important political posts held by military figures.

Two of the operational commands deserve special attention. The first is the Army Strategic Reserve (Kostrad), Suharto's power base as he rose to power in 1965–66. The other is Army Special Forces (Kopassus), headquartered in the capital. A plan was announced in June 1996 to expand Kopassus' force strength from 7,000 to 10,000 troops, but it is unclear how far the plan had advanced when the economic crisis hit in the summer of 1997. Kostrad and Kopassus are the best-trained and best-equipped troops in the Indonesian military, as well as the most mobile. Consequently, they are the most important both militarily and politically.[5]

The army also has an apparatus for territorial operations designed to mobilize people and resources to support guerrilla and internal security operations. All levels of the territorial command have an intelligence function, and all levels above the military subdistrict command have an intelligence staff that provides operational support for its own commanders as well as reporting nationally to BIA.

ELEVEN WHO REALLY MATTER

Because of the way in which it is organized, the military can effectively pursue a political course of action only if the 11 officers in the following positions come to a consensus on what that action should be: the commander-in-chief of the armed forces, the armed forces chief of the general staff, the armed forces chief of the social and political staff, the chief of the Armed Forces Intelligence Agency, the army chief of staff, the commander of the Army Strategic Reserve (Kostrad), the commander-general of Army Special Forces (Kopassus), the commander of the Jakarta Military Command, the navy chief of staff, the air force chief of staff, and the chief of the national police.

Within this group of military leaders, a core group of five carry the most clout: the commander-in-chief, the army chief of staff, and the commanders of the army's Strategic Reserve, Special Forces, and Jakarta Military Command. If they can agree among themselves on a political strategy, they will usually be able to impose their will on the rest of the military leadership.

Aware of the military's potentially powerful voice in political matters, Suharto took pains to ensure, especially in the past decade, that no such consensus would emerge among the top rank of officers. He loaded up the military leadership with officers he considered personally loyal to him and fostered rivalries between two main groups. A brief look at the incumbents as of March 1998 indicates some of the divisions within the military leadership, in particular between General

Wiranto, the armed forces commander, and Lieutenant-General Prabowo Subianto, the Kostrad commander and Suharto's son-in-law.[6]

At armed forces headquarters:

Commander-in-Chief General Wiranto, presidential adjutant, 1989–93

Chief of General Staff Lieutenant-General Fachrul Razi

Chief of Social and Political Staff Lieutenant-General Susilo Bambang Yudhoyono, Wiranto's close ally

Chief of Armed Forces Intelligence Agency (BIA) Major-General Zacky Anwar Makarim, Prabowo Subianto's close associate

At army headquarters:

Army Chief of Staff General Subagyo, presidential bodyguard, 1986–93, and a Prabowo ally

Commander of Army Strategic Reserve Lieutenant-General Prabowo Subianto, Suharto's son-in-law

Commander of Army Special Forces Major-General Muchdi Purwopranyoto, Prabowo's ally

Commander of Kodam X/Jaya (Jakarta) Major-General Syafrie Syamsuddin, presidential bodyguard, 1993–95, and Prabowo's ally

At other services:

Navy Chief of Staff Admiral Arief Kushariadi

Air Force Chief of Staff Marshal Sutria Tubagus

Chief of National Police General Dibyo Widodo, presidential adjutant, 1986–92

The two most important facts about this list are that it includes two former presidential adjutants, two former presidential bodyguards, and Suharto's son-in-law; secondly, the list reflects the intense rivalry between Commander-in-Chief Wiranto and Suharto's ambitious son-in-law, Lieutenant-General Prabowo.

Wiranto's main allies, who dominated armed forces headquarters, included Lieutenant-General Susilo Bambang Yudhoyono, armed forces chief of social and political staff; Major-General Agus Wijaya, assistant for general planning to the armed forces commander-in-chief; and Major-General Agus Wirahadikusuma, expert adviser on politics and security to the armed forces commander-in-chief. Meanwhile, Prabowo and his allies controlled army headquarters, as well as army operational commands headquartered in Jakarta. Given the divisions within the top leadership, it is not surprising that the military hierachy was never able to reach agreement to act independently of Suharto. Indeed, the military remained loyal to the president up to the last minute.

WINDS OF CHANGE

It was not only the very top of the military leadership that found itself politically hamstrung by Suharto. Since the early 1990s, rapid changes had been under way in the upper echelons of the army, especially among officers with the rank of colonel or above. Under Commander-in-Chief General Feisal Tanjung (May 1993–February 1998) frequent, large-scale personnel changes were a striking feature of military life. Major reshuffles took place in 1993, twice in 1994, three times in 1995, twice in 1996, and again in 1997, each involving more than 100, and sometimes more than 300, senior officers.

Several factors contributed to the waves of reshuffles. The first concerns enrollment patterns at the Indonesian Military Academy in Magelang, Central Java. For reasons that are not entirely clear, the academy produced many more army officers in the late 1960s and in the first half of 1970s than in later periods, as Table 1 shows:

Table 1. Cadets Graduated from the National Military Academy

Year	No. of Graduates
1965	433
1966	243
1967	203
1968	465
1969	no class
1970	437
1971	329
1972	389
1973	436
1974	434
1975	304
1976	85
1977	79
1978	93

Given that the number of higher-ranking positions in the military remains roughly constant, variation in the size of the officer corps has a direct, lasting impact on officers' prospects for promotion. The military leadership under Feisal Tanjung responded to the logjam in several ways. It sought nonmilitary assignments for officers on active duty and early retirement for officers deemed expendable. And it accelerated the transfer and rotation of officers, thus giving as many as possible a chance in the much-coveted command positions.[7]

The last response was carried out in the name of "regeneration," in Feisal Tanjung's parlance.[8] In 1969, the Military Academy switched from a three- to a four-year program. It appears that what Feisal Tanjung had in mind by regeneration was that academy officers born in the period 1946–52 and graduated between 1970–75 would be promoted to senior positions to replace officers from classes before 1969. Table 2 shows the distribution of officers by academy class as of March 1997.

As the table shows, thanks to Feisal Tanjung's regeneration, most officers graduating from the Military Academy in 1968 or before have been eased out, while officers graduating in 1970 or after now dominate the top reaches of the military.

There were also political calculations at work behind the regeneration campaign between 1993 and 1998. The rapid reshuffling of senior officers succeeded in purging from influential positions officers considered loyal to General Benny Murdani, the armed forces commander-in-chief from 1983 to 1988 and minister of defense from 1988 to 1993.

Table 2. The Class Distribution of Officers in the Top 55 Positions by Academy Class

Academy	Armed Forces HQ	Army HQ
1965	1	–
1966	2	–
1967	–	–
1968	1	2
1970	2	8
1971	1	10
1972	–	3
1973	1	1
1974	–	3
Navy	4	–
Air Force	2	–
Police	1	–
Unknown	3	10

Murdani, a powerful and controversial figure, fell afoul of Suharto sometime in the late 1980s, reportedly for encouraging Suharto to rein in his avaricious children.

The Presidential Palace was unsure how deeply "contaminated" the officer corps was when it embarked on a purge. Some army officers suggested that when Murdani left the government in 1993, perhaps as many as 50 percent of officers with the rank of colonel or above had direct links to him. Christian generals and intelligence officers became major targets in the purge because Murdani himself was a Christian and had spent much of his career in military intelligence.

INTRAMILITARY POLITICS

The purges were over by early 1994, and in the last four years, officers graduating from the Military Academy between 1968 and 1974—above all Wiranto, Susilo Bambang Yudhoyono, Subagyo, and Prabowo—were groomed as future military leaders.

A few caveats are in order before any discussion of cliques within the military. One is that it is very difficult to say how politically significant any particular group is. Secondly, it is worth noting that factional loyalties tend to shift over time, especially in a time of crisis. In Suharto's final days, however, the military seemed clearly divided into two competing factions.

After his appointment as armed forces commander in February 1998, Wiranto and his allies appeared to be largely in control of armed forces headquarters and a few army regional commands. Although he served as a presidential adjutant for five years and his loyalty to Suharto was unquestioned, Wiranto was, and is, considered a consummate military professional. He and like-minded officers were often referred to as "Merah Putih," which literally means "Red and White," as in the colors of the Indonesian flag. More broadly, it refers to officers intent on preserving the military's institutional autonomy and supportive of a secular state.

It should be noted that though Wiranto was considered loyal to Suharto, he did not have much experience as a senior military commander. He had served as commander of Kodam X/Jaya (Jakarta) for 15 months, commander of the Army Strategic Reserve for another 15, and as army chief of staff for 8 months before being appointed commander-in-chief. He has spent too little time in any one position to build a significant power base of his own.

Similar things can be said about Wiranto's most important ally, Lieutenant-General Susilo Bambang Yudhoyono, the chief of the social and political staff at armed forces headquarters since March 1998. He had risen through the army hierarchy in tandem with Lieutenant-General Prabowo Subianto in the previous five years.

Much has been said about Prabowo, one of the late New Order's most controversial figures. As the son-in-law of Suharto, Prabowo engendered a great deal of resentment as he rapidly rose through the ranks. As a military commander, Prabowo has been accused of human rights violations throughout his career. He was also considered politically ambitious. Prabowo and his classmate Syafrie Syamsuddin played key roles in the government's operation to evict supporters of Megawati Sukarnoputri from the office of the Indonesian Democratic Party in July 1996, an operation that sparked several days of rioting in Jakarta. More recently, Prabowo was accused of kidnapping and torturing political dissidents in early 1998.[9]

Prabowo, unlike Wiranto, Susilo Bambang Yudhoyono, and many other senior army officers, has spent most of his career with Kopassus, the Army Special Forces. After graduating from the Military Academy in 1974, Prabowo joined Kopassus and remained there until 1986, building up a solid power base along the way. He extended his influence during his tenure at the Strategic Reserve, Kostrad, from 1986 to 1993.

Prabowo's allies rose through the army hierarchy on his coattails. To understand how well positioned his group was, one need only look at some of his friends who served in strategic positions in and around Jakarta in 1997 and 1998. For instance, Major-General Zacky Makarim, a Class of 1971 graduate with extensive experience at Kopassus, has been chief of the Army Intelligence Agency (BIA) since August 1997. Prabowo's classmate Major-General Syafrie Syamsuddin, who also has a Kopassus background, was commander of the Jakarta Military District from September 1997 to June 1998. And Major-General Muchdi Purwopranyoto, a Class of 1970 graduate and another Kopassus stalwart, succeeded Prabowo as commander of army special forces in March 1998.

Although it is too early to say anything definite, intramilitary politics seemed to intensify early in 1998 as the economic and social crisis deepened. Wiranto and Susilo Bambang Yudhoyono opened channels of communication with students and intellectuals who were calling for Suharto's resignation and allowed them to organize protest rallies on campuses. At the same time, they warned the students not to bring their protests onto the streets, apparently fearing that street demonstrations might provoke riots, which in turn might force the military leadership into a bloody crackdown.

Prabowo, on the other hand, appeared to use the crisis to further his own political agenda. Although solid evidence is still lacking, some believe Prabowo instigated some of the anti-Chinese riots on the northern coast of Central and East Java early in 1998. As mentioned earlier, Prabowo was allegedly involved with the kidnapping and torture of pro-democracy activists at about the same time. More relevant to the final showdown in May, many observers believe, although again without solid evidence, that Prabowo had a hand in the killing of four students at Trisakti University on May 12 and in the rioting, looting, arson, and rape of Sino-Indonesian women in Jakarta the following three days.

Why would Prabowo involve himself in such crimes? First, he had attempted to cultivate popular support on an anti-Chinese, Islamic platform. He had long cultivated support among Muslim intellectuals affiliated with the Center for International Developmental Studies and the Indonesian Association of Muslim Intellectuals (ICMI) as well as with activists from the Indonesian Committee for Solidarity with the Islamic World (KISDI). All these groups contain elements who are considered highly critical of Indonesia's ethnic Chinese and Christian minorities.

Secondly, some believe Prabowo fomented the riots in mid-May to make Wiranto, his chief rival, look incompetent in the eyes of Suharto. According to this view, Prabowo hoped the unrest in Jakarta would convince Suharto to give him special powers to restore security and order.

In the end, it turned out that Suharto had much less confidence in Prabowo than the young general believed. The riots of May 13–15 brought the political climate to a boil and Suharto was forced to accept a program of political reform that included, among other things, a cabinet reshuffle, a new reform committee, and a pledge of new elections.

The military under Wiranto remained loyal to the president. On the evening of May 20, Suharto summoned Wiranto to his private residence and asked whether the military could maintain security and order. Wiranto said yes but added that there would be victims. Suharto chose not to test the military's resolve and resigned the following day. It is impossible to say how the military would have responded had Suharto given the order to repress the protest movement.

The Military in Transition

Once Suharto was gone, Prabowo was soon to follow. According to military sources, Prabowo met newly installed President B. J. Habibie on the evening of May 21 and demanded that the army chief, General Subagyo, be appointed commander-in-chief of the armed forces and that Prabowo himself become army chief of staff. But Habibie was neither able nor willing to protect Prabowo at the cost of alienating the military leadership under Wiranto. Early the following morning, Habibie asked

Wiranto to serve as his minister of defense and security as well as commander-in-chief of the armed forces. Wiranto in turn asked Habibie's approval for removing Prabowo as commander of the Army Strategic Reserve. The deal was struck.

What transpired on May 22–23 has been widely reported, and it should suffice to mention two important developments here. First, Wiranto ordered Major-General Johny Lumintang, his assistant for operations, to take over command of Kostrad from Prabowo in the early evening of May 22. Lumintang went to Kostrad headquarters alone in a jeep with his driver. Prabowo was not at the Kostrad headquarters when Lumintang arrived there. He got in touch with Prabowo by telephone and told him that he was taking over command. Lumintang then served as Kostrad commander for only 17 hours. He was replaced by Major-General Djamari Chaniago, who had served as an infantry division commander at Kostrad from August 1995 to August 1997 when Wiranto was Kostrad commander. The quick switch led to a speculation that Lumintang was replaced as Kostrad commander because he was a Christian, that Islamic groups opposed a Christian general in charge of the elite Army Strategic Reserve, and that Wiranto had backed down and appointed Djamari Chaniago as the replacement. With the evidence still in short supply, it remains unclear whether the opposition to Lumintang's appointment came from Islamic groups or, as some military sources suggest, from Feisal Tanjung, the coordinating minister for defense and security.

Second, shortly after he was ousted at Kostrad, Prabowo went to Habibie's house with Kopassus troops, presumably to demand once again that he be appointed army chief of staff and Subagyo commander-in-chief. But Habibie did not see him, military sources say. Habibie's expert adviser, Sintong Panjaitan, told Prabowo that Habibie was not available. Habibie was then airlifted to the Presidential Palace for safety, while the Kopassus troops under Prabowo returned to base in the early morning of May 23.

Army Chief-of-Staff Subagyo also played an important role in those crucial hours. Prabowo undoubtedly believed that Subagyo was on his side, demanding that Habibie appoint him commander-in-chief, but Subagyo in fact remained loyal to Wiranto, and although details remain unclear, he most likely took over Kopassus from Major-General Muchdi on Wiranto's behalf on the evening of May 22. Prabowo was thus left with a small number of Kopassus troops personally loyal to him, certainly not enough to turn the situation in his favor. He met with Wiranto on May 23, agreed to his new assignment as commander of the army staff and command school, and conceded defeat. In August, Prabowo was released from active duty after a hearing by a military honor council into the abductions of pro-democracy activists earlier in the year. At the time of this writing, it is unclear whether he will face a court-martial.

Subsequent developments led to the dismantling of Prabowo's power base in the army. As mentioned above, Major-General Muchdi Purwopranyoto was relieved of his command of Kopassus during the evening of May 22. Army Chief of Staff Subagyo held the command temporarily, and Major-General Syahrir was installed as the new Kopassus commander on May 25. The head of the Jakarta Military Command, Major-General Syafrie Syamsuddin, was replaced by a Wiranto ally, Major-General Djaja Suparman, on June 25.

Kostrad Chief of Staff Major-General Kivlan Zein was replaced by Major-General Ryamizard Ryacudu, the son-in-law of former vice president Try Sutrisno, and, it was unceremoniously announced, was to be seconded out of the army. Brigadier-General Idris Gassing was exiled to Irian Jaya as chief of staff of the provincial command based in Jayapura. Brigadier-General Eddy Budianto was relieved of his command of Korem 061 Bogor on May 29 and banished to the Secretariat of the West Java regional office of the National Security Coordinating Agency. Colonel Suryo Gino was sacked as Commander of Kostrad's 17th Infantry Brigade on June 4. Colonel Chairawan is under arrest for the part he played in the kidnapping of pro-democracy activists. Major-General Zacky Makarim, who heads the military's main intelligence unit, is one of the few who remain in strategic positions.

Should one conclude that Wiranto has been consolidating his control over the military and is emerging as a new military strongman? Yes and no. With the passing of Prabowo, there is no longer a rival power center in the army to challenge the military leadership under Wiranto. The commander-in-chief's power was also underlined by the replacement of Police Chief Dibyo Widodo by Police Lieutenant-General Roesmanhadi, who had served Wiranto as an expert adviser on security and social order.

On the other hand, the officers who replaced Prabowo's allies in strategic positions are not necessarily Wiranto's allies, with the notable exception of Djaja Suparman, the new commander of the Jakarta military garrison. Military sources say that Wiranto's group remains small and tightly knit; many of the junior officers who were close to Prabowo are uneasy with the military leadership.

Wiranto must also walk a fine line in the political arena. It will be a tricky task to balance his pledge on May 21 to protect Suharto with his responsibilities in what is supposed to be a reformist government that will restore popular confidence in the military as an institution. It is widely known that Wiranto has met with and received advice from Suharto several times since he stepped down; that Wiranto had the attorney general replaced in June, partly to protect his former boss; and that Wiranto wavered between Suharto's choice and Habibie's for the general chairman of Golkar in July.

It is not clear how long Wiranto is willing and able to walk the line. However much he wants to remain personally loyal to Suharto, his primary duty and loyalty are to the military, which has a host of problems clouding its long-term future. The military has lost much prestige and authority in the eyes of the public because of its inept handling of the violence in May 1998 and the breakdown of law and order that followed. It is also under strong public pressure to explain its role in past bloody confrontations, including the 1984 Tanjung Priok incident, the 1989 killings in Lampung, the dirty war in Aceh in the late 1980s and early 1990s, the protracted conflict in East Timor, and the mass killings in 1965–66.

The military leadership understands that the era of repression and state-sanctioned terrorism is over. Senior police officers, both retired and on active duty, are calling for the police to be separated from the military. Civilian forces openly question the military doctrine of dual function. The number of parliamentary seats to be allocated to the military will be reduced to 55 under the government's draft law on the legislature. The military may find its parliamentary presence reduced even further. Military leaders are unsure how to prepare for the coming era of party politics and have little to offer in dealing with the current economic crisis. It is highly unlikely, therefore, that the military under Wiranto will intervene in politics in a forceful way in the immediate future.

But this does not mean that the military is ready to go back to the barracks. Since its beginning, the military has always had a political role; and it has too much to lose, in terms of power, prestige, money, and self-esteem, at both the national and the local level, if it agrees to relinquish that role now. It wants to be part of any Indonesian government in the years to come, and it is safe to say that the military will not give up its political power without a fight.

The military retains enormous structural power. It still has a monopoly on the state's coercive power and still dominates Indonesia's intelligence community, however tattered the military may be in this time of crisis. And the military maintains its territorial apparatus, which can easily control the new political parties springing up. The military will remain in politics, and not a few officers will be waiting in the wings for their turn if Wiranto cannot deliver what officers deem themselves entitled to.

Notes

1. *Angkatan Bersenjata*, July 23, 1997.
2. Officers' social and political roles are not confined to those institutionalized under the dual-function doctrine. For instance, army officers act as fixers in business dealings, and soldiers moonlight as bodyguards.
3. The BIA was created in January 1994 to replace the more powerful Armed Forces Strategic Intelligence Agency, known as BAIS ABRI. At first it was headed by the assistant for intelligence to the armed forces chief of general staff, but the BIA chief gained independence in November 1995, reverting to the arrangement under BAIS ABRI. For more about BAIS ABRI and BIA, see The Editors, "Current Data on the Indonesian Military Elite: September 1, 1993–August 31, 1994," in *Indonesia* 58 (October 1994), pp. 84–85.
4. As of the end of 1997, 11 of the 15 top leaders at armed forces headquarters were army officers, while two were from the navy and one each from the air force and the police.
5. The position of commander of the army strategic reserve was upgraded from a two-star job to a three-star one in 1996, while the two divisional commanders under him were made major-generals. The position of commander of army special forces was upgraded from a one-star job to two stars, and its designation changed from commander to commander-general. It should also be noted that the Kostrad 17th Infantry Brigade and the Jakarta 1st Infantry Brigade under Kodam X/Jaya's commander, along with the Army Special Forces (especially Group IV and V) and the Marine 1st Infantry Brigade, are of strategic importance for the security of Jakarta.
6. For the timing of personnel changes, see The Editors, "Current Data on the Indonesian Military Elite: January 1, 1992–August 31, 1993," in *Indonesia* 56 (October 1993), pp. 119–52; "Current Data on the Indonesian Military Elite: September 1, 1993–September 30, 1995," *Indonesia* 60 (February 1996), pp. 101–46; and "Current Data on the Indonesian Military Elite: October 1, 1995–December 31, 1997," *Indonesia* 65 (April 1998), pp. 179–94.
7. See The Editors, "The Indonesian Military in the Mid-1990s: Political Maneuvering or Structural Change?" in *Indonesia* 63 (April 1997).
8. See *Forum Keadilan*, September 1, 1994.
9. For more about Prabowo and the kidnapping cases, see *D&R*, July 25, 1998, pp. 15–25, especially "Baret Merah: Satuan Pendadakan," pp. 24–25; *Adil*, July 22–28, 1998, pp. 4–7.

5

The United States, the IMF, and the Indonesian Financial Crisis

JOHN BRESNAN

THE LEADERLESS revolution that brought down President Suharto of Indonesia in May 1998 opened an era of great challenges for the world's fourth most populous nation as well as for the United States and the international community. The slow collapse of Suharto's 32-year rule as financial panic spread in Asia left Indonesia's economy severely depressed. Political institutions were without legitimacy. The military, students, politicians, and ordinary citizens had stepped back from the brink after three days of rioting in Jakarta, but social tensions continued to boil over on a smaller scale. Fixing these ills demanded major political changes at home and large-scale aid from abroad. The United States, motivated by its extensive economic and strategic interests in the country and the region, can help shape the world's response to Indonesia after Suharto, setting in motion positive trends across Southeast Asia.

Most observers now agree that Washington's reluctance to act to contain the Asian financial crisis soon after it began in July 1997 was an error. With the Thai baht plummeting after being floated by Bangkok, the United States remained on the sidelines as the International Monetary Fund (IMF) mobilized lenders for a $17 billion bailout of Thailand in August 1997. Throughout Asia, people criticized the United States, and Thais were shocked by the failure of a longtime ally to come to their assistance. The panic spread. When Indonesia requested IMF help in October 1997, the Clinton administration still hesitated to act. Stock prices fell dramatically on Wall Street and on exchanges from Hong Kong to Argentina. Only then did the administration alter course from the long American tradition of assigning Indonesia a low priority and from its more recent aloofness because of a fund-raising scandal involving the 1996 Clinton reelection campaign and an Indonesian businessman. In the end, the administration attempted the strongest U.S. intervention in the country in more than 30 years.

Many observers believe that the role the United States played and the remedies the IMF prescribed in Indonesia were mistaken. Granted, both were acting under constraints; U.S. policymakers had to contend with a fractious Congress, and the IMF was trapped by a history that did not prepare it for the new crisis of private capital. Both the United States and the IMF also lacked expertise on Indonesia that was adequate to the depth of intervention they attempted. In addition, then President Suharto of Indonesia was mistaken in thinking that he could avoid significant losses by his family and friends. The cost of these combined errors was enormous; the World Bank estimated that the turnaround in growth in Indonesia, from a positive 7 percent in 1997 to a projected negative 15 percent in 1998—a net loss of 22 percent—was the worst the world has seen since the Great Depression of the 1930s.

These developments in Indonesia demonstrated that U.S. policy toward that country and, more broadly, U.S. and IMF policy in the increasingly globalized economy, were in disarray. By October 1998, the crisis had reached Russia and Brazil, and was beginning seriously to affect the United States. The IMF itself was now the object of widespread criticism, and the United States was scrambling unsuccessfully to pull together an international consensus on what to do.

Whatever action the international community might take in time, the Indonesian experience has several inescapable lessons. Private capital markets are not self-correcting without potential costs that are unacceptable in the new global community. In particular, ways must be found to protect small economies from the potentially devastating effects of short-term capital flows. Both the United States and the IMF also need to find ways to remedy their lack of expertise on Indonesia—and on any other country in which they undertake to intervene as deeply as they have in this case.

The United States also faces a bilateral policy agenda on Indonesia that requires urgent attention now. The United States should be more generous in helping Indonesia deal with its unprecedented economic and social problems than planned U.S. resources will permit. At the same time, the United States should hold to the view that the successor

Habibie administration in Jakarta is a transitional one and should keep the pressure on for wider negotiation and debate on Indonesia's political future. The United States has an opportunity to influence that future in a more open direction, and that is an opportunity the United States should grasp.

The United States Acts

One has to go back more than three decades to find a president of the United States intervening in Indonesia's affairs in a manner comparable to that of President Clinton in February 1998. In the early 1960s presidents John F. Kennedy and Lyndon B. Johnson both sent then Attorney General Robert F. Kennedy to Jakarta to change the mind of President Sukarno, once about dropping his threat to invade Western New Guinea, the second time about ending his confrontation with Malaysia. Neither mission was successful.

By the 1990s, geoeconomics had supplanted geopolitics in East and Southeast Asia; the enemy was not a foreign military power but a roiling of financial markets. The panic that began in Bangkok on July 2, 1997, spilled into the rest of the region. On October 26, when Secretary of the Treasury Robert E. Rubin ruled out an Asian bailout led by the United States, he nevertheless had reason to do so. The $40 billion bailout of Mexico in 1994, led by the United States, with the IMF in a supporting role, had been highly controversial. (The administration avoided the need to obtain Congress's agreement by drawing on a little-known Treasury fund for currency stabilization; Congress promptly clamped limits on the fund's use.) Now Congress was considering legislation to replenish the IMF and pay arrearages due the United Nations, two politically sensitive goals important to the administration. Also pending was legislation to extend the president's "fast-track" authority to negotiate international trade agreements, which the White House sought in order to expand the North American Free Trade Area southward beyond Mexico. Rubin had grounds for avoiding anything that smacked of the Mexican bailout.

But the day after Rubin's statement, October 27, stocks on Wall Street fell 554 points, or 7 percent, in the 12th worst day on record, forcing the New York Stock Exchange to suspend trading. Stock prices dropped in Hong Kong, Japan, and Europe, slid further the next day in New York, then followed suit in Brazil and Argentina.

Responding to the swiftly widening panic, the Treasury let it be known on October 30 that the United States would commit $3 billion as a "second line of defense" to support an IMF-led rescue plan for the

Indonesian economy. The offer, U.S. officials said, was designed to address "market contagion"—"the odd ways in which a loss of investor confidence in one nation spreads to others." Mindful of the fallout from Mexico, the officials pointed out that the roles of the United States and the IMF were reversed from those in that bailout and noted that the Fund's money would come with strings attached, including measures to root out the nepotism and corruption that supported the business interests of Suharto's family and cronies. U.S. officials added that they did not expect Indonesia even to need to draw on the U.S. funds.

Thus the United States was out in front of the IMF in Indonesia, despite its original intentions. In the formal announcements by the two on October 31, Rubin said: "Financial stability around the world is critical to the national security and economic interests of the United States. These countries are not only key markets for U.S. exporters, but are also crucial to our efforts to promote growth, peace and prosperity throughout the world."

Shoring up Indonesia looked like a good bet. Experts considered its economy fundamentally sound and noted that the country was already taking significant steps to calm its markets, calling on the IMF more as a confidence-building measure. Moreover, Suharto selected Widjojo Nitisastro, chief architect of the country's long run of rapid economic growth and well known to international financial institutions, as the lead Indonesian negotiator in talks with the IMF.

Indonesia also bulked very much larger than Thailand. It had a population of 200 million, its economy was the largest in Southeast Asia before the crisis hit, and U.S. economic interests there were its largest in the region. Rubin could, moreover, convincingly invoke national security. Indonesia was primus inter pares in the region politically; its support was essential to any serious undertaking in Southeast Asia. Under Suharto, it had helped ensure that the first-ever organization of the nations of East Asia (the Asia Pacific Economic Cooperation forum) would include the United States rather than exclude it, as Malaysia had urged. Jakarta undertook significant roles in many other regional disputes, including in Cambodia and the South China Sea. Moreover, no China policy was thinkable without the balance that a strong Indonesia brought to regional affairs. On the other hand, an Indonesia in disarray could pose a regional danger, as one literally could see in 1997 across much of Southeast Asia, where a haze created by hundreds of Indonesian forest fires was threatening the health and economies of a half dozen countries.

Whether the United States was right to join the intervention in Indonesia, however, depended on whether or not the intervention was effective. And that, in turn, depended on whether the IMF had the right remedy and whether Suharto would take it as prescribed.

The Right Medicine?

Although the details of the October 31, 1997, letter of intent from the Indonesian government to the IMF, specifying what Indonesia would do in return for financial support, were not made public at the time, the document called for government spending cuts and the closing of banks deeply in debt. Two lines of criticism arose immediately.

One critique, made in the November 3 *New York Times* by Jeffrey D. Sachs, director of Harvard University's Institute for International Development, maintained that the IMF was applying remedies it had developed in its past work with countries that had been living beyond their means and printing money to make up the difference. But such remedies, he said, were inappropriate for the Southeast Asian economies with their budget surpluses, low inflation, and, until recently, stable or rising foreign exchange reserves. The problem was a 1993–96 "lending binge" by international money market managers and investment banks, with the borrowed funds going for investments in real estate and other nonexporting sectors. "This year, the bubble burst," declared Sachs. He said the IMF was pressing Asian countries to jack budget surpluses still higher, tighten domestic bank credit, and close weak banks that had been caught up in the boom-bust cycle of foreign lending.

Off the record, Fund officials conceded that they were groping for an appropriate response to a new phenomenon. The closure of 16 banks in Indonesia touched off a run on all domestic private banks and dried up much of the domestic credit supply. Within months, the IMF had to ease the terms it had imposed on both Indonesia and Thailand, allowing them to run budget deficits instead of surpluses. Working against the success of the intervention, both the Fund and the Treasury lacked Indonesian expertise among their staffs, which became a more important factor as they reached more deeply into Indonesia's affairs.

Some observers in the private financial markets in Jakarta took a different tack from Sachs, arguing that the letter of intent did not go far enough in sacrificing the interests of Suharto's family and friends. The agreement did not deliver a coup de grace to the controversial national car project in which President Suharto's son Hutomo (Tommy) Mandela Putra had an interest. Nor did it end government subsidies to such state-owned enterprises as aircraft manufacturer Industri Pesawat Terbang Nusantara (IPTN), Research Minister B. J. Habibie's pet project.[1]

Such reforms would not directly affect the flow of capital in the short term, but corruption and nepotism were leading factors in Indonesia's economic problems. If they were untouchable, this group of critics said, it was doubtful that Suharto would make any of the other hard decisions necessary to resolve the financial crisis.

At this time, many observers were perplexed by the inchoate character of U.S. policy. President Clinton neglected to make the U.S. position clear when he met privately on November 24 in Vancouver with President Suharto. The editor of the *Far Eastern Economic Review* wrote at about the time of that meeting that Clinton had been "a distant president for most of Asia and for Southeast Asia in particular." As a Democrat, he did not inspire liking in many Asian elites, with their Republican sympathies. Unlike George Bush, who was a familiar figure in the region before being elected president, Clinton was largely unknown in Asia when he entered office, and many there regarded his election as a "recipe for trouble."[2] Clinton's "retreat from leadership" was particularly pronounced in his handling of Indonesia. "Paralyzed" by the Indonesian campaign contributions scandal,

> Clinton let relations fester. Protesting the administration's criticism of Indonesia's human rights policy, Jakarta canceled an agreement for military cooperation with the United States and an order for F-16 fighters. Not until Clinton's belated appointment (in mid-1997 after a six month vacancy) of Stanley Roth as assistant secretary of state for East Asian and Pacific affairs and Roth's forceful advocacy of a more proactive policy toward Indonesia did Clinton attempt to halt the slide.[3]

Perhaps the combination of this president's unaccustomed reticence as scandal swirled around him and the famous reluctance of Treasury Secretary Rubin to speak his mind contributed to the lack of clear American leadership early in the Asian financial crisis.

The Quiet before the Storm

After the government closed the 16 banks in early November 1997, unnatural quiet prevailed in Jakarta. For two entire months, no initiatives were forthcoming from the government. Suharto appeared in public only rarely, raising fears that no one was in charge as well as speculation about the successor to the then 76-year-old president. In December the IMF reportedly sent him a strongly worded letter about carrying out promised policy changes.

In early January 1998, Suharto announced a 1998–99 budget that was widely considered overly optimistic. Indonesia's currency and stock markets suffered their worst one-day losses ever, and there was panic buying in the shops, motivated by fears the IMF would cut off assistance. In the United States, amid expectations that American corporations would increasingly feel the pinch of a slowdown caused by deterioration in Asia, the Dow Jones industrial average fell 2.85 percent in one day, its steepest drop since the plunge in October. In one week, stocks fell 14 percent in Hong Kong, 23 percent in Singapore, and 19 percent in Manila. Alarm bells were ringing again in Washington and other capitals.

President Clinton telephoned Suharto on January 8 while aboard *Air Force One.* Clinton made it "quite clear that the IMF program has to be followed," according to a high administration official, and also told the Indonesian president that he was sending a delegation of senior officials to the region in the next several days, led by Lawrence H. Summers, deputy treasury secretary. In addition, Defense Secretary William S. Cohen stopped in Indonesia on a previously scheduled tour.[4] Prime Minister Goh Chok Tong of Singapore, whose government had matched Japan's commitment of $5 billion to the IMF program, paid a personal visit. In telephone calls to Suharto, Prime Minister Ryutaro Hashimoto of Japan and Chancellor Helmut Kohl of Germany, among others, emphasized the importance of conforming to IMF norms.

Stanley Fischer, senior deputy head of the IMF, said the Fund would "like to accelerate the program and strengthen it, because a lot of people believe the Indonesian government isn't really committed to the program."[5] He pointed out that two closed banks with ties to Suharto family members were back in business in a matter of days. A confidential IMF report distributed to members castigated the Suharto government.

Under intense pressure from abroad and pushed by his own chief negotiator, Widjojo, to accept reforms, President Suharto signed a new letter of intent with the IMF on January 15 that called for wide-ranging austerity measures aimed at halting the economic slide. As Suharto affixed his signature, IMF managing director Michel Camdessus stood over him, arms folded across his chest, looking every inch the schoolmaster he was playing in the drama. The photograph of this scene became a symbol of the charged issue at the heart of the negotiations—whether the IMF, and through it the United States, had the right to dictate terms to the Indonesian government in return for help in restoring confidence in its economy.

The second agreement worked from the sobering assumption that the economy would register zero growth in 1998–99.[6] Unlike the first agreement, which had called for a government budget with a surplus of 1 percent of gross domestic product (GDP), this pact allowed Indonesia to run a 1 percent deficit, making possible increased spending to stimulate the economy. The government was to reduce subsidies, however, and to allow prices for food and fuel to move upward.

The pact also mandated numerous structural reforms that many observers found breathtaking because of the extent to which they would reduce the wealth and power of Suharto family members and associates if carried out. Budget and off-budget funding of the aircraft manufacturer IPTN was to stop. Every form of support was to be withdrawn from the national car project. Bank Indonesia, the central bank, was to be given full autonomy to set monetary policy and interest rates. Many government monopolies and cartels were to be eliminated, such as those for sugar, wheat, and paper, although not the one for rice.

Mohammad Sadli, an Indonesian economist and former cabinet minister, wrote that the agreement "exceeds the wildest expectations of economists and other intellectuals who had demanded reforms during the past few years but could not get very far against an overwhelmingly strong government bent on keeping the status quo." But there were many skeptics who doubted Suharto would allow real reform.[7]

Five days after the signing, President Suharto let it be known that he was ready to serve a seventh term and indicated that his candidate for vice president and potential successor was B. J. Habibie, a longtime cabinet favorite and family friend best known for his eccentric views on economic policy and his championing of extravagant high-technology projects. The rupiah, having traded at 2,400 to the dollar the previous July, fell to 17,000 to the dollar, making it the world's worst performing currency. The market, it seemed, did not like Indonesia's prospective leadership.

The succession to the leadership looms large in any system in which regular open elections are not held, especially regimes built around one authoritarian leader who, like Suharto, had presided over a long period of rapid economic growth. Camdessus had raised the issue of presidential succession with Suharto, probably limiting himself to suggesting that an early indication of Suharto's plans would help calm markets. U.S. Treasury officials are said to have threatened to cut off U.S. support altogether if Habibie became vice president. Was Suharto challenging the United States? One Suharto confidant, no friend of Habibie, said that the Americans, by opposing him so strongly, had given Suharto reason to prefer him. But while Habibie was not esteemed by the Americans, he was well regarded in Germany, where he had been educated, and in Japan, where his preference for protectionist policies was accepted. In addition, he appealed to Suharto because he had no political base of his own. And because the military did not like him, his presence in the vice presidency could help forestall the likelihood of a coup. Suharto, an adept balancer, had tapped Habibie to protect himself. He probably calculated, too, that the Treasury was bluffing. He gambled that Indonesia was too important for the United States to cut off, and he won.

Doing Something

Perhaps because Suharto discovered that his signing the agreement was widely seen as capitulating to the IMF, he took no vigorous steps to implement it. The one economic issue that he attended to was the languishing of the rupiah, which hovered in the vicinity of 10,000 to the dollar. Suddenly he developed an enthusiasm for the controversial idea of a currency board that would limit the domestic money supply to the country's foreign currency reserves at a fixed rate of exchange against the U.S. dollar. The central bank and the Finance Ministry learned about the plan from newspapers, as did the IMF and the U.S. government. Camdessus publicly declared that he had written Suharto to say that if the government set up a currency board, he would recommend discontinuing the bailout.

At this pass, the White House decided to send former vice president and ambassador to Japan Walter Mondale to Indonesia to try to get through to Suharto. President Clinton had telephoned the Indonesian president twice in one week to keep him from committing to the currency board idea. By now there had been four such calls, described by a senior U.S. official as "unsatisfying at best." The January meeting of Lawrence Summers and Suharto had been a 90-minute monologue—"classic Suharto," in one official's words.

Mondale had a 90-minute meeting with Suharto on March 3. The Indonesian president told him that he was being "victimized." What the United States and the IMF were demanding was "suicide." Hours later, Lawrence Summers told senators that the White House could not support additional IMF aid for Indonesia unless Suharto made "adequate progress" on reforms agreed to in January. Nevertheless, the administration hesitated, fearing that any food riots or other outbreak of violence in Indonesia would be blamed on the Fund and the United States.

Also on March 3, Bank Indonesia reported foreign reserves of $16.3 billion, down 25 percent from the close of 1997. The year-on-year inflation rate in February was 31.7 percent, nearly double January's. Foreign sources in the banking industry said the central bank was flouting the IMF by pumping funds into inefficient local banks to keep them alive.

On March 6 the Fund said it was delaying the infusion of $3 billion slated for March 15 because the "basic conditions" of the agreement had not yet been met.

As scheduled, on March 11 President Suharto was unanimously reelected to a seventh five-year term in an impressive display of his personal control of the formal levers of power, and Habibie was elected vice president. On March 14, Suharto announced his cabinet, which confirmed rumors circulating before Mondale's visit about cronies hostile to the agreement with the IMF becoming ministers. The new minister of finance was Fuad Bawazier, a former tax official known as an associate of Suharto's children. Minister of trade and industry was Mohammad "Bob" Hasan, the head of the plywood cartel and Suharto's golfing companion. Minister of social affairs, charged with overseeing relief, was Siti (Tutut) Hardiyanti Rukmana, Suharto's eldest daughter. By now Suharto also had downgraded Widjojo and fired the central bank governor.

The cabinet may have been intended partly as a snub to the IMF and the United States, but it mainly demonstrated that Suharto was showing his age, retreating further into a small circle of family and friends whom he felt comfortable with and thought he could trust. That was the only positive thing one could say about the new cabinet. It was the least competent Suharto cabinet so far. And it left the government without lines of communication to key domestic constituencies.

On April 8, a month after the new cabinet's installation and three weeks after the arrival of IMF negotiators, the parties agreed on a third pact, which highlighted the cost of Suharto's dispatch of his experienced economic team. The new government was being put on a short leash. The document included a long list of commitments and target dates for action. There would be, an American official said, "step-by-step monitoring" and doling out of money in small amounts as the government acted on its commitments.

The Indonesian president did not have much choice by this time, with pain and frustration rising in the country. As this IMF agreement neared completion, the Fund expected Indonesia's economy to shrink by 5 percent in calendar year 1998, compared with the January expectation of zero growth. Annual inflation was projected at 47 percent, compared with a January estimate of 20 percent.[8] Meanwhile, the newly unemployed in Indonesia were estimated at 5.5 million, and their number was expected to climb to between 8 and 9 million by year's end. Moreover, the ranks of the underemployed, constituting 41 percent of the workforce of nearly 90 million in 1996, were expected to increase drastically. Up to this point, student protests had been limited to university campuses, but they were becoming more violent. If they moved off the campuses, where they could be joined by unemployed youth, the violence would ratchet sharply upward.

Two fundamental issues were finally addressed in the third round of IMF talks: restructuring of the domestic banking industry and resolution of the foreign debt of Indonesia's private corporations. What was happening with the domestic banks was not entirely clear. In agreement with the IMF, the government had created the Indonesian Bank Restructuring Agency (IBRA) in January to take over control of banks that were seriously overextended. By early April the IBRA had 54 banks under close supervision; some 250 examiners were placed in these banks to monitor compliance with restrictions on new credit and payments of dividends, but experienced examiners were in short supply. In late April the rating service Standard & Poor's (S&P) fixed the money put into the banks in the form of low-interest government loans since the crisis began at $10 billion. While 23 banks had been closed in the previous six months, 200 or more were still operating, and analysts believed most of them would not be viable. Nonperforming loans would reach 55 percent nationwide by the end of the year S&P estimated. Apparently no one in the central bank was prepared to take on the well-connected owners of the private banks. This differed markedly from the situation in Thailand and Korea, where new governments were dealing with their financial institutions with a good deal more authority. The banking sector in Indonesia cried out for a new government with a firm hand.

Resolution of the foreign indebtedness of Indonesia's private corporations was no less important as the key to restarting the flow of foreign capital. Bank Indonesia reported a figure of $80.2 billion for private foreign loans as of April 3, 1998. At prevailing rates of exchange, the Indonesian firms could not or would not pay their debts. Steering committees of representatives of the Indonesian corporations and the foreign banks had been meeting in Singapore and elsewhere in search of a solution to the problem. The IMF, perhaps with an eye to the free-market lobby in the United States, did not make the resolution of this indebtedness a formal part of its discussions with the Indonesian government until the negotiations leading to the third agreement. By then the IMF could not avoid concluding that the government must take an active role if the problem was to be solved. Various sources were reported as saying that the resolution plan would include features of a model used in Mexico, with the government selling foreign exchange to debtor corporations at a predetermined rate for the exclusive purpose of repaying their foreign debt. But a full-fledged plan to deal with the foreign private debt problem was thought to be weeks or months away.

Suharto had ignored the existence of a crisis after reaching the first agreement with the IMF and had tried to blackmail the IMF with the currency board scheme rather than implement the second agreement. Now a month had been taken up with negotiating the third agreement with a new Indonesian team. Five months had passed, and there were few results to be seen except the continued downward spiraling of all the economic indicators.

Frustration and Fall

The April 8 IMF agreement provided for an enormous intrusion into the governance of Indonesia that was more readily compared with Fund dealings with postcommunist Russia than with Latin American countries. More than 100 policy reforms had target dates for action. A monitoring system was to be established to track structural reforms. Indonesia's ineffective bankruptcy law was to be amended and a special court established to deal with claims. Seven state enterprises were to be privatized within a year. The list ran on and on.

By this time, U.S. officials dealing with Indonesia were extremely frustrated. Treasury officials urging that Congress approve an additional $18 billion for the IMF were criticized fiercely at an April 21 House Banking Subcommittee hearing for "funding a vicious dictator." Indonesia certainly stood out in the Asian crisis. Suharto was saying there could be no political change until 2003, while new leaders in Thailand and South Korea simultaneously strengthened democratic institutions and pursued economic reforms. U.S. officials rightly worried that the world increasingly saw them as propping up the Suharto dictatorship by continuing economic aid. And it was possible the whole IMF effort could collapse if the mounting criticism by Indonesia's students burst beyond the campuses and the military used violence to suppress it. But the alternative was to deny the aid and directly contribute to a mass outbreak of violence. "The Indonesian people—particularly the poorest—have a tremendous interest in seeing financial stability restored," David Lipton, the undersecretary for international affairs at Treasury, said. "And so do we."

But financial stability was not to be. A May 4 increase of 70 percent in the price of gasoline by the wealthy and corrupt state oil company led thousands of people in the city of Medan in North Sumatra to rampage through the streets for three days. Then students in Java began to move off their campuses. The IMF had pressed for an end to subsidies by October but gave the government leeway to go about it as it thought best. Most sources agree that Suharto approved the fateful price increase personally; that he was overconfident seems plain. He was also under strong pressure to act. Only hours after the announcement in Jakarta of the gas price rise, the IMF released the long-delayed first tranche of $1 billion. In the United States, the Export-Import Bank approved loan guarantees worth $1 billion to enable Indonesian factories to buy American materials they needed to begin working again.

At the same time, the Pentagon canceled a joint training exercise with the Indonesian Armed Forces. The United States had circumstantial evidence that elements in the Indonesian Armed Forces were kidnapping and torturing political dissidents. That Washington had not broken off ties with the Indonesian military earlier is an indication of the caution with which it was dealing with Suharto. The U.S. ambassador to Indonesia, J. Stapleton Roy, called on several Indonesian army leaders as early as late February to express his concern about such reports. In the weeks that followed, at least four of the young activists were transferred to police custody. The chief suspect in the disappearances was Major-General Prabowo Subianto, a son-in-law of Suharto, and a potential future powerholder himself. Many doubted that it was possible that the armed forces leadership, and Suharto himself, were not aware of the kidnappings.

By the second week of May, thousands of students were battling with police and armed forces in cities and towns in many parts of Indonesia and calling for Suharto to step down. On May 12 the flashpoint was reached as security forces in Jakarta shot and killed four students and wounded at least a dozen others when they fired live ammunition at demonstrators who spilled out of a college campus onto a major highway. Concerned that the United States was still too closely identified with the Indonesian president, the State Department issued a statement that deplored the killings and for the first time agreed with critics that Indonesia was in need of "political reform."

There was an outpouring of anger over the students' deaths, and a chaos of rioting, looting, and burning (and, as later came out, raping) engulfed the city on May 13–15, with the loss of something on the order of 1,200 lives. President Clinton said, "I strongly urge the Indonesian government to initiate quickly a dialogue on reform with its citizens. Giving the people of Indonesia a real voice in the country's political affairs can make a real contribution to restoring political order and stability based on human rights and the rule of law."

The Clinton administration was immediately under pressure from Democrats in Congress to intervene directly in Indonesia by exerting pressure on Suharto to leave office. Assistant Secretary of State Roth said on May 18 that the administration did not want to "stir the pot in a very tense situation and possibly get an outcome we don't want." The administration, he said, also would not spell out the kind of political reforms it believed should take place in Indonesia, because "these are things the Indonesians have to work out." On May 19 Suharto proposed fresh elections but failed to name a date and was seen in Jakarta as stalling yet again. Secretary of State Madeleine Albright, in a speech on May 20, said of Suharto: "Now he has the opportunity for an historic act of statesmanship—one that will preserve his legacy as a man who not only led his country, but who provided for its democratic transition." This statement was widely seen as a call for Suharto to step down. By this time, Suharto was already preparing to resign.

The United States was undoubtedly right to delay expressing an opinion about Suharto's tenure in office. It was important for the Indonesians to manage their political crisis with a minimum of outside involvement. And it was prudent for the United States to remain aloof from premature identification with any of the competing Indonesian interests. What would happen after Suharto's departure was not known. It was highly unlikely that common sense should have prevailed as thoroughly as it did in Jakarta in May 1998—a tribute to the practical wisdom of a large proportion of the national elite. The violence might well have been much more widespread. It might have left civilians and the armed forces pitted against each other or even have resulted in a military junta's taking power. That it led to a continuing and broadening jockeying for power was an unexpectedly healthy outcome.

With regard to economic policy, however, the United States and the IMF had some reevaluating to do. The Treasury had held that economic stability would contribute to political stability, but instead political change turned out to be essential to economic stability. The proposition that the Suharto government could work its way out of the crisis with IMF help, a reasonable risk at first, had become more and more dubious as the months passed. The Indonesian president, who had made many hard decisions over the previous three decades, was unable to do so in 1998. In the end, the IMF did the only thing left to it: it starved the Suharto regime of cash.

The crisis in Indonesia continued to worsen as of this writing in October 1998, a year from the start of IMF intervention. The Indonesian currency was still only a third of its precrisis value, and only the first steps were being taken to restructure the banking system and the private sector's massive foreign debt. Economic output was expected to fall in 1999 as well as 1998, and tens of millions of Indonesians had already become unemployed. Inflation was more than 80 percent and rising, while the price of rice had tripled. More than half the children under two on the populous island of Java were suffering from malnutrition, and there was widespread looting of businesses, plantations, and rice warehouses. International agencies were expecting nearly 50 percent of the population to have fallen below the poverty line by the end of 1998 and for the number to rise further in 1999. Antagonistic crowds forced Habibie to cut short a visit to Surabaya, the second largest city in the country. Officials were under pressure in many localities to resign. The Habibie administration proposed fresh parliamentary elections in June 1999 and presidential elections in December 1999, but there was concern whether public order would permit that schedule to be kept. Even martial law was viewed as of doubtful efficacy, owing to a precipitous decline in public regard for the armed forces as a result of their accumulated abuses.

The Indonesian catastrophe had multiple causes. Foreign investors imprudently put money at risk in the economy in search of higher rates of return. Domestic businessmen imprudently invested short-term loans in long-term ventures, particularly real estate. The government of Indonesia did not have systems in place to monitor these developments. The IMF had gotten off to a damaging start that actually made the situation even worse. The United States attempted to play a decisive role but lacked the financial and political resources to match that ambition. Suharto greatly aggravated an unpromising situation by his absorption with the welfare of his family and friends. The weakness of neighboring economies, especially the inability of Japan to serve as an engine of regional growth, aggravated conditions in Indonesia. By October 1998, Indonesia was hurtling toward a future that one could view only with profound pessimism.

Larger Questions

As important as the IMF remedies were to a resolution of the Asian monetary crisis, public debate in the United States was not concerned primarily with the efficacy of the programs imposed on the several countries. Discussion of whether the IMF had been right in raising interest rates and trying to hold down budget deficits was limited to professional economists. The questions that engaged policymakers in Washington were larger ones.

The debate might be said to have begun on January 21, 1998, when Treasury Secretary Rubin, in a speech at Georgetown University, defended the Clinton administration's efforts to quell the financial turmoil in Asia. By this time Korea had joined Thailand and Indonesia in turning to the IMF for help. While the effects of the crisis on the United

States had been relatively limited thus far, Rubin said, the financial instability could spread to other nations and eventually derail the long economic expansion and stock market boom that many Americans were enjoying. Alan Greenspan, chairman of the Federal Reserve, agreed. Before spring was over, he told a Senate committee, the falling currency values in Asia, "will be showing through here in reductions in demand for our exports and intensified competition from imports." Economic activity could moderate from its recent brisk pace. While such a slowdown "would appear helpful at this juncture," growth in the United States might slow too much if the crisis spread. As Greenspan said a day later in testimony before a House committee, there was "a small but not negligible probability" that Japan, Latin America, and Eastern and Central Europe could suffer "unexpectedly negative effects," with repercussions felt in the United States and elsewhere.

For the first months of the Indonesian crisis, the U.S. stock market boomed as if Asia would not affect it. In early April 1998 the Dow Jones industrial average closed above 9,000 for the first time, then stalled and fell amid growing concerns about the turmoil in Asia. In March the Commerce Department reported that the trade deficit soared in January 1998 to its highest level in a decade as the crisis in Asia depressed demand for American goods. Corporate profits dropped in the fourth quarter of 1997. By June 1998, the Japanese economy was in recession, Russia was appealing for more help from the IMF, Hong Kong's economy was in trouble, labor problems were occurring in Korea, and markets were down in Germany, Brazil, and Mexico.[9] In June, however, Alan Greenspan said the U.S. economy was "enjoying a virtuous cycle" in which rising stock prices encouraged spending and growth, and he suggested the possibility that the economy had "moved beyond history." Such official optimism did not exactly motivate Congress to look favorably on IMF funding. Not until October 1998, after Russia had defaulted and Brazil was appealing for IMF help, did Greenspan concede that the likelihood of good times in America had "weakened considerably."

The lack of pressure on the American economy, coupled with the optimism of U.S. officials, also gave critics of IMF action in Asia ample time to organize. Three prominent free-market proponents, George P. Shultz, William E. Simon, and Walter B. Wriston, declared that it was "the IMF's promise of massive intervention that has spurred a global meltdown of financial markets." What should have been done was to "let the private parties most involved share the pain and resolve their differences." The IMF must be stopped, or "further bailouts, unprecedented in scope, will follow."[10] At least a small group in Congress shared the trio's confidence in the ability of financial markets to sort themselves out. The group included key figures in the House of Representatives like the majority leader, Republican Dick Armey of Texas. Anyone familiar with the damage the financial markets had helped wreak in Indonesia, however, might have been less optimistic.

A narrower conservative position was that the IMF was right to intervene in the Asian countries but wrong to impose structural and institutional reforms. In an article in *Foreign Affairs,* Martin Feldstein, a Harvard professor of economics and former chairman of the Council of Economic Advisers, charged the IMF with "overdoing it" in East Asia. By imposing reforms, as opposed to focusing on balance-of-payments adjustments, he said, the IMF would discourage governments from turning to it in a timely manner. However, while disbanding Indonesia's monopolies and cartels would not directly restart the flow of international capital into the country, the market saw it as a test of Suharto's willingness to make the hard decisions necessary to stabilize the economy. Furthermore, it is unlikely that any American government would have risked $3 billion of taxpayers' money in Indonesia without assurances that the arrangements benefiting Suharto's family and friends would be substantially curtailed.

The U.S. interest in structural reforms to improve the quality of governance was not new; they had been a part of World Bank programs for years. What was new was the imposition of such reforms by the IMF during a crisis when the international community's leverage was at its peak. But if not then, when?

Liberal critics took the opposite tack, saying that the IMF should make a condition for its help that the Indonesian government also improve political, religious, and workers' rights, and conditions in East Timor. In a letter to President Clinton, 27 members of Congress, including Michigan's David Bonior, the second-ranking Democrat in the House, demanded these conditions and threatened to oppose increased American funding of the IMF. But these critics ignored the fact that the IMF was already making substantial political demands on the Suharto government. Adding this group's demands might have ended all possible IMF influence in Jakarta.

Democratic critics also found fault with the IMF proposal to amend its charter to allow the Fund, when studying a country's economy, to examine its openness to all types of investment. These critics viewed the proposal as a means of promoting the unrestricted movement of capital into and out of countries. The House Democratic leader, Richard A. Gephardt of Missouri, and five senior colleagues threatened to withdraw support for President Clinton's request for new financing for the IMF because of concern that the charter proposal failed to attend to the need to mitigate the human consequences of financial globalization. Here the critics could certainly cite the Indonesian case as an example. Indonesia was wide open to capital flows; indeed, one would have thought that was part of its problem.

Still others took the view that the United States should seek nothing less than Suharto's removal. This view was put forward by activists in Indonesia, by such publications as the *New York Times* and the *Economist*, and by Georgia Republican Newt Gingrich, then Speaker of the House of Representatives.[11]

Should the United States have tried to bring down President Suharto? Could it have? Had the United States halted the IMF program with the selection of Habibie as Suharto's successor, the Indonesian Army would not have withdrawn its support of Suharto. Had protests grown larger, military leaders would probably have ordered troops to fire on unarmed demonstrators and been obeyed. Only overwhelming crowds might have persuaded the army to tell Suharto to step down. While this is what eventually occurred, it would have been irresponsible for the United States to have tried to precipitate such a situation. The resignation came unexpectedly, before support coalesced around a candidate to succeed Suharto; as this is written, the succession is still in process. In these circumstances the United States could not have removed Suharto or put a successor in his place.

The United States could have taken a less cautious stance toward Suharto. Paul Wolfowitz, who served as assistant secretary of state for East Asian and Pacific affairs, ambassador to Indonesia, and undersecretary of defense for policy in the Reagan and Bush administrations, argued in an article in the February 5, 1998, *Wall Street Journal* that Suharto "must widen the base of his government by reaching out to critics and disaffected elements." Had the United States seriously pursued this line of thinking with the Indonesian president, it might have helped avoid the trauma that occurred. But no one in the administration had Wolfowitz's first-hand experience or the confidence that flowed from it.

With this exception and that of the issue of unhindered capital flows the situation in Indonesia did not support any of the courses of action critics of the IMF proposed. The critics did, however, reflect the wide array of opinion on the Asian crisis. And the combination of the attacks on the U.S. administration and the IMF from the right and the left achieved several results. In the House of Representatives, support for IMF replenishment was delayed, putting the IMF management on notice to take its critics seriously. The critics also, by putting the administration and the IMF on the defensive, made it difficult for them to look beyond Suharto. It was not an edifying example of U.S. foreign policy development.

Finance ministers attending IMF and World Bank meetings in Washington in October 1998 failed to reach agreement on a course of action. Only when turmoil in finance markets signaled that the crisis was having a ripple effect on the United States—the value of the dollar fell, the U.S. bond market dropped, and hundreds of stocks plunged on the New York Stock Exchange—did administration officials and congressional leaders say they were hopeful they could agree on compromise legislation to provide $18 billion to refill the IMF's reserve accounts, which had been depleted by the Fund's attempts to bail out the economies of Thailand, Indonesia, Korea, and Russia.

What America Should Do

Suharto's fall offered a new beginning for U.S. policy in Indonesia. What role should the United States play in the restructuring of Indonesia's political and economic life?

The United States has a strategic interest in Indonesia being a stabilizer in Southeast and East Asia and the Pacific rather than, as at present, a destabilizing force. It has an interest in an Indonesia that is a positive force in the recovery of the East Asian economies rather than, as at present, a drag on its neighbors. And it has an interest in an Indonesia that comes through its transition from authoritarianism with a government that has broad popular support and is accountable for its actions.

As this is written in October 1998, none of these Indonesias was assured. The cohesion of the nation-state was threatened for the first time since the 1950s, as autonomy was proposed for East Timor and leaders elsewhere talked of autonomy or independence for their regions. Meanwhile, in the capital, the elite were just beginning to refashion their political ideas and institutions. And the economy continued its headlong rush toward disaster.

Some 40 million Indonesians were vulnerable to food shortages because of high inflation, a low exchange rate, and loss of jobs. If the economy continued to decline at its current pace, observers feared, further rioting might well break out and martial law be declared. Indonesia required humanitarian, economic, and election aid on a large scale. Some believed balloting in the next year could turn Indonesia into the world's third largest democracy. The stakes were high.

The United States needed to formulate a coherent policy on Indonesia and stop relying on the ad hoc reaction to events that had marked its behavior through most of 1998. The White House needed to coordinate

American policy more actively; allowing the Treasury, the State Department, and the Pentagon to pursue their separate agendas had sown confusion about U.S. priorities and intentions.

A coherent U.S. policy for Indonesia would begin with helping to alleviate the worst suffering from the economic collapse. The food shortage was fundamental: the country needed to import more food than it could now afford to buy, and unemployed people needed money to buy food they could no longer pay for at market prices. That large-scale food riots had not yet occurred by October 1998 was something of a surprise and a tribute to the extended family as a social security system. But the prospect of millions of poor people suffering as a result of a monetary crisis whose origins lay outside the country as well as within it called for a larger U.S. response. Much of the world looks to the United States to set the standard for humanitarian action.

But aid on the scale required into 1999 and beyond will not be possible so long as the U.S. foreign aid budget, adjusted for inflation, remains the smallest it has been in 25 years. And repair of that deficiency is remote with the Clinton White House and the Republican Congress locked in an impeachment contest. The United States thus stands to cede its leadership in humanitarian concerns to others. In Indonesia and in Southeast Asia more generally, the limited ability of the United States to provide assistance at this time of greatest need is likely to be seen as a failure of the American political system and one more sign of declining American political commitment to the country and region.

The United States also should be working on an urgent basis with the international financial institutions to help Indonesia restructure its domestic banking system and with the other G-7 governments, especially Japan, to structure a solution to Indonesia's private foreign debt. The IMF was much too slow in putting these tasks on its agenda and has since been approaching them with too little urgency. Yet both must be addressed if there is to be even the beginning of a return to normalcy in the financial sector of the Indonesian economy. These are practical steps that need to be taken as quickly as the Indonesian authorities can be moved to take them.

There is a question of what assistance the United States and the rest of the international community should be making available to the Indonesian government prior to the holding of acceptable elections. Many in Jakarta consider the Habibie administration as lacking the legitimacy to govern, and Habibie himself has acknowledged the seriousness of the problem by his agreement to fresh elections to Parliament and the presidency. Some in Jakarta have been opposed to any foreign aid, saying it would only redound to Habibie's credit and help him in his evident efforts to retain the presidency. Moderates have insisted that the economic crisis cuts too deeply to permit partisanship to determine support for the maintenance of essential public services that Indonesia can no longer afford from tax revenues. These opponents of Habibie also have in mind that any lessening in the severity of the economic crisis would give the government that emerges after him a better start on the task of economic recovery. The United States would do well to adopt these moderate views. At the same time, the United States must make it clear to Habibie that it considers him only a transitional figure in the absence of credible elections.

The IMF made known that the $43 billion for the Indonesian bailout would not be enough and some $6 billion more had become necessary; no one could say for certain, either, that this would be the last time the figure would rise. Yet the donor governments among the industrial democracies would have to take into account Indonesia's reputation for widespread corruption and unearned wealth, especially when it came to Suharto's family and friends. It is possible that a significant portion of this wealth is already hidden outside the country and that what remains behind is greatly depreciated in value. In addition, investigation into how the elite has acquired those assets would take time and money and, as the Philippines' experience with former President Marcos' wealth has shown, might yield only limited results. Nevertheless, any government of Indonesia must, as a matter of public ethics, try to recover as much of the Suharto family's ill-gotten wealth as it can. The United States should make progress here a condition of further financial commitments to Indonesia.

Foreign aid is only a temporary fix for what troubles the Indonesian economy in any case. Any aid will fall far short of replacing the private capital, domestic and foreign, that has fled Indonesia and must be attracted back if the economy is to recover. It seems unlikely that the Habibie administration can make much headway in this regard, since economists regard the caretaker president as eccentric in his economic thinking and private businessmen regard him as unfriendly to the marketplace. Many from both groups whom the writer interviewed in June 1998 not only consider Habibie corrupt but see his cabinet as including anti-Chinese racists.

Chinese-Indonesians were traumatized by the rioting, looting, arson, and raping to which they were subjected during the three days in May 1998. Some who could afford it scattered as far as Perth, Australia, and Portland, Oregon, in search of counseling. Tens of thousands who fled to Singapore and other refuges in the region stayed put. Thousands more still in Indonesia were making plans to leave. But most Chinese-

Indonesians could not leave; their future would depend on how the indigenous majority decided to deal with them. Many indigenous Indonesians also were shaken by the violence, which revealed a racism they had failed to acknowledge as endemic to their society. The problem is plainly deep-seated and will require long-term attention by national leaders. In the meantime, measures must be adopted that give Chinese-Indonesian businesspeople a sense of security. Foreign investors are not likely to return to Indonesia in any numbers while local investors hold off resuming business activity. The donor community has every reason to require continuing attention to this problem as a prerequisite for economic aid.

Indonesian elections should be a matter of great interest to the United States, considering the priority in foreign policy that the Clinton administration has given political rights. Habibie has proposed draft legislation for new elections to Parliament in June 1999 and to the presidency in December 1999. There was a notable lack of consultation in the drafting process with actors outside the Habibie administration and the armed forces. The United States should insist that the electoral process be designed with full participation by all the major political actors expected to take part in the elections.

There are questions of how elections are to be financed, whether seats are to be reserved in Parliament for the armed forces, and who should oversee the process and certify the results. The United States has had considerable experience with elections in transitions from authoritarianism around the world but would be wise to eschew a leading role here; it is too convenient a target for political fringe groups in Indonesia. At the same time, the internationalization of the elections would help assure their fairness. Thais, Filipinos, and Koreans in particular could share the fruits of their experiences. The United States could help ensure that the elections take place under acceptable circumstances by taking steps to create an intergovernmental contact group on the elections comparable to the intergovernmental group that worked so effectively on the currency board threat.

With Indonesia at this juncture dependent on the international community, the issue of East Timor was bound to come to the fore. For some time Indonesia had been prepared to grant autonomy to the former Portuguese colony in return for international recognition of Indonesian sovereignty there. Habibie made the offer public in June 1998, and it was welcomed by some leaders in East Timor and in exile. But some East Timorese were not prepared to concede sovereignty and demanded a referendum on the question and the swift withdrawal of Indonesian troops in the meantime, as the soldiers appeared unable to maintain order without shooting and killing local youths. Complicating movement on the issue of East Timor, many in the Indonesian elite have long accepted the official view that Indonesia was responding to the East Timorese when it invaded and annexed this small, defenseless neighbor. Nor was it clear that independence without some form of association with Indonesia would be in the interests of East Timor, which has very limited natural and human resources. The U.S. position was to acknowledge Indonesian control, while maintaining that a valid act of self-determination had not taken place. The United States should be advising the Indonesians that only a U.N.-brokered agreement will satisfy world opinion.

The United States must also clarify its policy toward the Indonesian Armed Forces. The Pentagon played a rearguard role during the long process in which U.S. support to the Indonesian military was reduced under congressional pressure—cutting off sales of small arms that could be used against civilians and then watching as Indonesia, to save face, canceled the purchase of F-16 aircraft and access to U.S. military training institutions. Unknown to Congress, U.S. troops continued secret joint training exercises with the Indonesian military, principally involving the special forces of the two nations. The Indonesian Special Forces were led for many years by Prabowo Subianto, the son-in-law of Suharto, who had received training in the United States and was something of a darling of the Pentagon. His ambition, however, fomented a major split within the Indonesian military that apparently contributed to its ineffectiveness in the rioting of May 1998. Indonesia is in the process of reassessing the armed forces' role in the country's political life. It is time the United States made a reassessment of its own. The United States should support a continued role for the armed forces in the governance of Indonesia if that is what a credibly elected government of that country decides. But the resumption of joint programs should be calibrated to the satisfactory completion of investigations of alleged abuses.

The United States should be prepared for the possibility of further large-scale violence in Indonesia. If it occurs, the United States should independently assess the need for martial law. The assessment of neither the Habibie government nor the Indonesian military leaders should be taken at face value. Both face potentially harsh judgments as the political system evolves and investigations of abuse and corruption multiply: self-interest could well count significantly in any decision to interrupt the political process. The possibility also cannot be ruled out that an overextended military could lose control and Indonesia's national cohesion begin to weaken seriously, starting in eastern Indonesia, which was left out of the economic boom and is likely to feel left out of the emergency relief.

The problems of Indonesia are fundamentally political, and they can be addressed only by political means. It may be necessary to respond to emergency conditions with police power in limited areas for brief periods of time. But army suppression of political activity may well have run its course as a useful tactic in Indonesia. It is in the interest of regional stability that Indonesia not begin to fragment or implode. These days, only a broad-based coalition of national unity seems likely to assure that. The Wolfowitz advice to Suharto—that he broaden the political base of his government by reaching out to critics—was even more applicable to Habibie.

The United States is ill-favored to play a strategic role with regard to Indonesia. No senior person in any department of the administration has lived and worked in Indonesia. The official U.S. presence in the country is relatively small. Congress has been otherwise occupied and, as this is written, is caught up in the impeachment process. Washington must rectify the problem of its limited contact with, poor intelligence on, and unauthoritative analysis of Indonesia; to do so, it must reach outside its own ranks.

The experience with Indonesia also demonstrates that the United States needs a new strategy to deal with the new problems resulting from the global movement of capital. If enormous future bailouts are to be avoided, ways must be found to reduce the volatility of short-term capital flows in the international financial system. An economy as vulnerable as Indonesia's needs protection from massive short-term capital flight, and the United States and the IMF should be thinking about what form this could take. Improved monitoring is a necessary element of any plan, as Treasury Secretary Rubin has suggested. But this is a long-term response. International monitoring can be no better than the monitoring by individual governments. And the long delay in getting a handle on the banking situation in Indonesia suggests how difficult reform will be. Attention also must be given to constraints on the short-term movement of capital that governments may introduce for their own protection. The exuberance followed by panic among money managers in the Asian crisis makes clear that the financial markets are far from perfect and cannot be relied on exclusively.

Demanding structural reforms of the government of Indonesia was an inevitable task for the IMF if it was to design a way out of the crisis that would merit international support. It is possible that some future governments in crisis will fail to come to the IMF in a timely fashion, fearing that the political cost will be higher than they are prepared to pay. But it is not unreasonable to expect that a concern for issues of governance, common in World Bank programs for some years, become an active concern of the IMF as well. While the United States is pondering changes in the IMF charter, it should consider introducing language that would give the IMF a mandate to take issues of governance into account as a regular part of its activity.

Beyond these fundamental positions it is unwise for the United States to venture. The fall of Suharto was a matter properly left to the Indonesians. The putting in place of a legitimate successor regime should be left to them as well.

Notes

1. John McBeth, "Big Is Best: Indonesia's Rescue Package Draws on the Thai Experience," *Far Eastern Economic Review,* November 13, 1997, pp. 68–69.
2. Nayan Chanda, "A View from Asia," *Foreign Policy,* Winter 1997/98, p. 66.
3. Ibid., pp. 67–68.
4. David E. Sanger, "Clinton Phones Suharto, Insisting on Commitment to IMF Plan," *New York Times,* January 9, 1998.
5. Seth Mydans, "Markets Tumble and Rumors Sweep Indonesia Capital: Panic Buying in Shops: Fears of IMF Aid Cutoff Stir Talk of Political Instability and Suharto Succession," *New York Times,* January 9, 1998.
6. The following account is drawn from "Isi Nota Kesepakatan IMF-Pemerintah Indonesia" [Contents of the IMF–government of Indonesia agreement], *Kompas,* Jakarta, January 16, 1998.
7. Mohammad Sadli, "Letter from Jakarta: The New IMF Agreement: A Necessary but Not Sufficient Condition for Exchange Rate Stabilization," *Indonesia in the United States: A Newsletter of the United States–Indonesia Society,* Winter 1998, pp. 4–5.
8. Jay Solomon and I Made Sentana of Dow Jones Newswires, with contributions by Kate Linebaugh, "Tentative IMF Deal Lifts Hopes That Rescue Will Resume," *Asian Wall Street Journal, Weekly Edition,* April 6, 1998.
9. Timothy L. O'Brien, "A Frenzy of Global Anxiety Kicks Up Dust That Had Been Settling," *New York Times,* May 28, 1998; Bloomberg News, "Market Falls Again, Ending Worst Month since October," *New York Times,* May 30, 1998.
10. *Wall Street Journal,* interactive edition, February 3, 1998. For a more extensive treatment of their argument, see the statement by Charles W. Calomiris of the Columbia Business School before the Joint Economic Committee of the Congress, February 24, 1998.
11. In an interview, Gingrich said: "In Indonesia there have to be clear negotiated mileposts for each tranche. Unless there are serious, step-by-step,

measurable, visible signs of change we are not going to help you because an unreformed, corrupt Indonesian government is going to absorb all the money we send and still not solve the problem." Advised by his interviewer that the matter was complicated by "the uncertainty of succession, like President Suharto stepping down," Gingrich replied: "Maybe that should be our goal." Interview by Nayan Chanda, "Strings Attached," *Far Eastern Economic Review,* February 25, 1998.

About the Authors

JOHN BRESNAN is a Senior Research Scholar of the East Asian Institute of Columbia University. He is the author of *From Dominoes to Dynamos: The Transformation of Southeast Asia,* published by the Council on Foreign Relations Press in 1994, and *Managing Indonesia: The Modern Political Economy* (1993) and the editor of *Crisis in the Philippines: The Marcos Era and Beyond* (1986). At Columbia University, he has served as the Executive Director of the Pacific Basin Studies Program, Adjunct Professor in the School of International and Public Affairs, and Co-chair of the University Seminar on Southeast Asia in World Affairs.

ROBERT W. HEFNER is Professor of Anthropology and Associate Director of the Institute for the Study of Economic Culture at Boston University. His most recent books include the edited volumes *Market Cultures: Society and Morality in the New Asian Capitalisms* (1998) and *Democratic Civility: The History and Cross-Cultural Possibility of a Modern Political Ideal* (1998). He is currently completing a book on Islam and democratization in the Suharto era.

R. WILLIAM LIDDLE is Professor of Political Science at Ohio State University and a specialist on Southeast Asian, particularly Indonesian, politics. His recent scholarly publications include *Leadership and Culture in Indonesian Politics* (1996); "The Islamic Turn in Indonesia: A Political Explanation," *Journal of Asian Studies* (August 1996); and "Coercion, Cooptation, and the Management of Ethnic Relations in Indonesia," in Michael Brown and Sumit Ganguly, eds., *Government Policies and Ethnic Relations in Asia and the Pacific* (1997). His Indonesian-language writings have been collected in *Islam, Politik, dan Modernisasi* [Islam, politics, and modernization] (1997). Professor Liddle has served as Chair of the Southeast Asia Council of the Association for Asian Studies and as Assistant Editor for Southeast Asia of the Association's *Journal of Asian Studies.*

JONATHAN PARIS is a Fellow at the Council on Foreign Relations specializing in the Middle East and Indonesia. He has been Visiting Lecturer at Yale University and has written articles on Indonesia, including

"Step by Step towards Indonesian-Israeli Relations," *Israel Affairs* (Winter 1996); and "Minority Rules: How Indonesia's Chinese Can Survive," *The New Republic* (July 13, 1998). His initial contact with Indonesia began in the early 1980s at the international law firm of Coudert Brothers, where he specialized in commercial and banking transactions in Indonesia. Jonathan Paris received a B.A. in political and economic systems at Yale and a J.D. from Stanford Law School.

ADAM SCHWARZ is a lecturer at the School of Advanced International Studies at Johns Hopkins University and at Georgetown University. He also consults for private firms and government agencies on the politics and economics of Southeast Asia. He was the 1997–98 Edward R. Murrow Press Fellow at the Council on Foreign Relations. He spent the previous decade in Southeast Asia reporting for the *Far Eastern Economic Review*. He is the author of *A Nation in Waiting: Indonesia in the 1990s* (1994) and "Indonesia After Suharto," *Foreign Affairs* (July/August 1997). Adam Schwarz received a B.A. in economics from Duke and a graduate degree in business from Columbia.

TAKASHI SHIRAISHI received his Ph.D. from Cornell University, taught at the University of Tokyo (1979–86) and Cornell University (1987–96), and is currently a professor at the Center for Southeast Asian Studies at Kyoto University. He also serves as Editor of the journal *Indonesia*, published by the Cornell Southeast Asia Program. His publications include *An Age in Motion: Popular Radicalism in Java, 1912–1926* (1990, awarded the Ohira Memorial Prize); *Indonesia: Government and Politics* (1991, in Japanese, awarded Suntory Prize); *Sukarno and Suharto* (1997, in Japanese), and *Network Power: Japan and Asia* (1997, with Peter Katzenstein).

Index